CASES IN INDIAN MANAGEMENT

A-SELECTION

CASES IN INDIAN MANAGEMENT

A-SELECTION

Dr. Bal Chansarkar

M.Sc., M.A., Ph.D., FRSS MMRS.

Himalaya Publishing House

ISO 9001:2015 CERTIFIED

First Edition : 2008
Second Edition : 2010
Edition : 2015
Edition : 2020

Published by : Mrs. Meena Pandey for **Himalaya Publishing House Pvt. Ltd.,**
Ramdoot, Dr. Bhalerao Marg, Girgaon, Mumbai - 400 004
Phone: 022-23860170/23863863; **Fax:** 022-23877178
E-mail: himpub@bharatmail.co.in; **Website:** www.himpub.com

Branch Offices :

New Delhi : Pooja Apartments, 4-B, Murari Lal Street, Ansari Road, Darya Ganj, New Delhi - 110 002.
Phone: 011-23270392, 23278631; Fax: 011-23256286

Nagpur : Kundanlal Chandak Industrial Estate, Ghat Road, Nagpur - 440 018.
Phone: 0712-2738731, 3296733; Telefax: 0712-2721216

Bengaluru : Plot No. 91-33, 2nd Main Road, Seshadripuram, Behind Nataraja Theatre, Bengaluru - 560 020.
Phone: 080-41138821; Mobile: 09379847017, 09379847005

Hyderabad : No. 3-4-184, Lingampally, Besides Raghavendra Swamy Matham, Kachiguda, Hyderabad - 500 027. Phone: 040-27560041, 27550139

Chennai : New No. 48/2, Old No. 28/2, Ground Floor, Sarangapani Street, T. Nagar, Chennai-600 017. Mobile: 09380460419

Pune : First Floor, Laksha Apartment, No. 527, Mehunpura, Shaniwarpeth (Near Prabhat Theatre), Pune - 411 030.
Phone: 020-24496323, 24496333; Mobile: 09370579333

Lucknow : House No. 731, Shekhupura Colony, Near B.D. Convent School, Aliganj, Lucknow - 226 022. Phone: 0522-4012353; Mobile: 09307501549

Ahmedabad : 114, SHAIL, 1st Floor, Opp. Madhu Sudan House, C.G. Road, Navrang Pura, Ahmedabad - 380 009.
Phone: 079-26560126; Mobile: 09377088847

Ernakulam : 39/176 (New No. 60/251), 1st Floor, Karikkamuri Road, Ernakulam, Kochi - 682011. Phone: 0484-2378012, 2378016; Mobile: 09387122121

Cuttack : New LIC Colony, Behind Kamala Mandap, Badambadi, Cuttack - 753 012, Odisha. Mobile: 9338746007

Kolkata : 108/4, Beliaghata Main Road, Near ID Hospital, Opp. SBI Bank, Kolkata - 700 010, Phone: 033-32449649; Mobile: 07439040301

DTP by : HPH Editorial Office, Bhandup (Archana)

Printed at : Trinity Academy, Mumbai. On behalf of HPH.

Preface

This book of 'Cases in Indian Management: A selection' is an outcome of the demand for case studies which meet specific requirements – both for teaching and learning. It is aimed at bridging the current gap for substantive cases, especially for higher management programmes.

A brief introduction to the use of case study approach both for teaching and learning is included for the reader to grasp what is necessary for using cases for teaching as well as for writing case analysis paper.

The first case 'Information and Library Services-A Problem of Resource Allocation' by B A Chansarkar, pertains to information and library services of a large (educational) institution. It deals with allocation of resources to meet dissatisfied demand along with the human resource problem of handling a delicate issue.

The second case 'Demand forecasting' by B A Chansarkar, deals with forecasting market demand for a well established company operating in the western region of India. The problem of market estimation (trend estimation techniques) and expansion through franchising forms the main thrust of the case. The case is designed to teach market estimation for a time series data for an established company over a long period time.

The third case 'Indian Aviation Sector' by S Mishra, studies the Indian aviation industry. It studies the current situation of Government airlines – Air India and Indian Airlines which is undergoing a rapid expansion and facing competition from the fast enlarging private airlines. It highlights the problems- mainly financial and human resource management. It should be of great use in strategic decision making in fast moving industries.

The fourth case 'Jagrut Grahak Mandal- Patan' by J Pancholi and A Modi, emphasizes on management accounting system of a non-government organisation (NGO) which is operating into voluntary service sector in the western part of India. It analyses the management accounting practices of an NGO and tries to highlight the intricacies of an NGO's responsibility towards its stakeholders such as donor, members, regulator authorities and the society at large. It introduces contemporary model of the Balanced Score Card.

The fifth case 'Succession Planning in Family Business – The Gender Angle: The Case of Mehta Steel' by B M Kacholia, deals with the situation about succession in a family business when the only member is a female. With business-owning families getting smaller in size and daughters getting good education, the business aspirations of female children are also rising and thus gender succession is gaining imoprtance.

The sixth case 'New Corporate Issues in Indian Agriculture' by R Singh, evaluates the common thread of integrating and tightening the supply chain among the collaborative partnership of Indian Corporate and rural India. In India due to legal restrictions on contract farming, this is a relatively new area of research, especially when the government is toying with the idea of bringing out legislative changes to facilitate contract farming and vertical co-ordination in agriculture. Mahindra's Shubhlabh service rallies Kisan Kendra, ITC e-Chaupal, and Kisan India.com are new agribusiness models, which are based on vertical co-ordination between Indian corporate and Indian farmer. This case evaluates three such attempts by corporate India i.e. PepsiCo's contract farming in Punjab, ITC's e-Chaupal and Mahindra Shubhlabh services.

The seventh case 'MTNL at a Crossroad' by M Chaturvedi, deals how an Indian public sector undertaking (PSU) in telecom sector responded to the competitive forces when globalisation, privatisation and liberalisation hit the market and the economy. It deals with various problems a PSU faces and the strategy adopted to meet these problems and the challenges.

The eighth case' The Dubbawallas of Mumbai' by A Rangnekar, deals with a unique robust model for delivery of house cooked meals at lunch in Mumbai. It highlights the strategic options needed to adjust to declining volume mainly due to suburban migration of offices, increasing meal time eating out and depleting manpower in this profession.

The cases are written by experts in their particular areas of specializations bringing out the basis and the complexities of the situations as dealt in real life. The book should form a basis for using cases in various aspects of management programmes. More cases of similar nature are planned for the future.

Bal Chansarkar
Editor
January, 2008

About Authors

Dr B A Chansarkar, MSc (Statistics), MA (Economics), PhD is currently a Visiting Professor at Middlesex University Business School, London. He worked as Senior Market Research Executive, Watney Mann Ltd, London for seven years. He has traveled to China, Japan, Poland, Hungary, Canada, USA and other European and Middlesex East countries for establishing management programmes. He has taught to Doctoral students in several countries. He has written number of books and published in International Journals.

Mr R M Chaturvedi, is presently working as General Manager in MTNL, Mumbai looking after the areas of Business Development and Corporate Customer Management. He is a graduate in Engineering and Law, and Post Graduate in Management from Jamnalal Bajaj Institute of Management Science. He has done Post Graduate Diploma in Investment and Market Studies and is presently pursuing Ph.D. in Management from NMIMS University, Mumbai. He has 25 years of diversified experience in various areas of Telecom Management including projects, planning, operations, logistics and strategic management and has worked in Gujarat, Madhya Pradesh and Mumbai.

Dr B M Kacholia, MBA in Marketing from Michigan University, USA and a PhD in Economics. He is a highly qualified Professional Manager with 30 years of experience of working as a senior executive in the Birla Group. He has served on the Board of Directors of a Public Limited Company for many years. After his retirement from Birlas, he initiated a unique one-year week-end Diploma Programme in Management of Family Business at NMIMS University. He is mainly engaged in teaching as well as research in the area of Management of Family Businesses.

Dr. Sita Mishra is a strong proponent of andragogy as a prerequisite for developing educational leadership through efficient academic delivery. She has taught marketing courses in various Management Institutes in Delhi. In her previous stint, she also worked in Marketing Division of Steel Company thereby helping herself in her endeavor to impart an even better learning experience to her students. Her research interests include consumer behaviour, retail marketing and rural marketing. She has written several research papers and has contributed over the years towards management education, research, training and managerial skill formation in India.

Dr. Ashwin G. Modi is a faculty member at the S K School of Business Management, Hemchandracharya North Gujarat University, Patan, Gujarat, India, a well known management institute India. Dr. Modi has published & presented many articles and research papers in national and international conferences. He is also a social activist and the secretary of Jagrut Grahak Mandal since 2000, a SEBI approved NGO & District Consumer Information Center.

Dr Jatin Pancholi B.Com, MBA, PhD is currently a Senior Lecturer at Middlesex University Business School, London. His area of interest is Activity Based Costing,

Balanced Score Card, Measuring Business Performance, Depository system and financial management. His works are also into entrepreneurship, management pedagogy, clusters and sustainable development. He is involved actively as an editor, member of the editorial boards and member of the advisory committees of few international and national journals, corporate and non-profit organizations in various capacities in India, UK and USA.

Dr Amit Rangnekar, MBA Mumbai University, has been working for over fifteen years in responsible positions in pharmaceutical industry. He has completed his PhD from Narsee Monji Institute Management Studies (NMIMS) University, Mumbai.. His interests involve key dynamics and demographics affecting global pharmaceutical strategy and performance.

Dr Rakesh Singh, Msc (Economics), PhD. Professor of Economics, NMIMS University. His areas of research are supply chain management, Business forecasting and strategy. He has published two books and several papers in national international journals.

CONTENTS

AN ESSENTIAL PART OF CASE STUDY APPROACH*

Dr B A Chansarkar
Middlesex University Business School, London, UK.

Case Study Method of Teaching

A case is a short description, in words and numbers of a typical management decision situation. Each case confronts the student with an actual or imaginary (but in the realm of possibility) management problem as that problem had/would have confronted by a manager at some point in its evolution. A case, thus, offers an easy transition from the text book theory to real-world application and simultaneously provides an opportunity to apply one or more principles found in the management textbooks.

The case method can be used at one end, for the fresh (that is, raw and inexperienced) management students, as well as for more experienced practicing managers, attending ad-hoc seminar or a well organized management development programme (a common practice now a days), both internal and external to the organization.

At the lower level, the students lack experience in applying analytical techniques, preparing the case for class discussion and written case assignments: the students may come poorly prepared with superficial analysis of facts and many will not have spent enough time on the assigned case. Hence, at the lower level, simple cases which are good for the situation analysis and problem identification are recommended.

More complex and rigorous cases involving formulation of alternatives, evaluating them and making recommendations can be used in the higher level management courses or in advanced development programmes. The more experienced the participants are, the more they are likely to get out of the case discussion method. This is more so when used for continuing education of practicing managers, who can draw a great deal on their higher conceptual level and individual experience, thus enriching the discussion level and benefiting from sharing mutual experience.

Advantages of Case Discussion

There are five main advantages of case discussion.

First, it allows principal application of conceptual knowledge.

- Academic (both theoretical and conceptual) knowledge is necessary but not sufficient for management decision-making and problem-solving business situation.

- Adapted from 'Case Method of Teaching in Management Education and Development: A Concept Paper', Dr. V. Patankar, Research Monograph No. 2, NMIMs, January , 2000.

- A case provides the students of management with the opportunity to apply their knowledge of management concepts and fundamentals, to a variety of real management problems.
- Students develop skills in applying concepts and techniques to real-life business problems in a classroom environment rather than merely learning them from textbook examples which are often very different from real-world situation. They bridge the gap between academic analysis and practical application of knowledge.
- Students are more likely to remember ideas and concepts that they themselves have evolved and used during the 'experience' of solving real-world problems.
- Case discussion is more interesting than pure lectures and textbook courses, because it demands more intensive and direct involvement in the learning process. Case method enhances the learning and practice of management.
- Students learn how to develop new concepts as well as to apply established concepts.

Second, it develops problem solving ability.

- Students learn to appraise the case situation, develop and evaluate various courses of action and select the best decision alternative. In addition, they have to defend their decision in the class.
- A case enables the students to use their knowledge and skills, to identify the problem, analyses alternative courses of action and develop strategies to address the diverse problems and opportunities that face the managers.
- Students learn to organize facts, then interpreting them in the from of relevant conclusions. They also learn to evaluate and interpret quantitative data that they would be expected to, in an actual business situation.
- Students learn to identify key problems and to differentiate between symptoms and problems. They learn to reason better, through the use of problem-solving approach.
- A case study method provides students with the opportunity to acquire skills for solving business/management decision-making.

Third, it provides experiential learning in creative atmosphere.

- Case method is experiential learning. It is the best method to make managers look at the organization in its totality and as a group of different unrelated functions like marketing, production, finance, personnel, etc.
- A case deals with problems of high relevance to organizations, at a level designed to challenge student's analytical and creative skills.

Fourth, it prepares students for doing research.

- A case develops student's ability to interpret the environment, using tools of research and logic, and to develop effective strategies and policies, based on that interpretation.
- A case emphasizes the use of the research data for managerial decision.
- A case encourages students to distinguish between good and unreliable research, relevant and irrelevant facts.

Finally, it enhances managerial skills.

- Students understand the importance of implementation as a necessary extension to sound decision-making.
- The group work and interaction among students, prepare them for the human side of management.
- Students improve their communication skills, both oral and written, necessary in their future career. They learn by exploration, discussion and even arguments.

In addition, a case discussion makes teacher's job more challenging and enjoyable though a lot of time and thought is often required to develop a case study.

However, there are limitations is using a case study method. Some of these are:

- It is the author of the case and not the student who has actually collected the facts in the organization concerned by the case. This makes lot of difference in understanding and appreciating the finer points of the case. Much depends on the case writer's ability to grasp the crucial facts and record them in an unbiased manner and clarity.
- The student does not have to implement his decision and live with the consequences, after having studied and discussed the case. Some participants, it is argued, would actually behave quite differently is discussing a case, if they knew that they would be responsible for implementing the conclusion. In real-life situation, a person may decide to live with the problem, but the same does not pertain to the case method.
- An open environment in the industry should exist, so that the information is shared and good case can be developed; many teachers are forced to use cases given in foreign textbooks, under environment totally different from that existing in our country. In such situation, the students are not able to identify themselves if the case environment is completely alien.

Role of the Instructor in a Case Class

Instructor plays various roles in the case discussion class – a leader, discussion leader, coach, teacher, timekeeper, synthesizer and a summariser. The instructor should be aware of these roles and should play the appropriate role when the situation demands.

(a) Case discussion class as a democratic process.

The case discussion method is a democratic process where the students and teacher have an equal, though different, role to play. The teacher must respect the students and their individual views, however, crude and radical they may be.

The teacher must approach the students, as a student himself/herself, who is equally keen to add to his knowledge from the case discussion. The teacher, however, experienced he/she is, cannot m atch the cumulative experience of the class of practicing managers. The teacher should create condition in which the rich experience can be shared.

(b) Directive vs. Non-directive method.

The degree of direction the teacher exercises is a point often debated. This, of course, depends on the objectives, on the student's readiness to accept the responsibility and the on the character and the content of the case at hand, as is seen in the following able.

Variable	More teacher directed	More student directed
Time in course	Early	Late
Teachers' purpose	To illustrate a concept	To encourage the students to develop concepts
Student's level of preparation	Students unprepared	Students well prepared
Student's stage of experience	Inexperienced students	Advanced and post-experience students.
Nature of case	Unstructured or hidden structure	Fairly obvious structure.

In a completely non-directive method, the teacher plays no or very small part, usually sitting at the back of the class and allowing the students to direct discussion among themselves without interruptions. The students give either individual or group presentations and even the leadership role is played by the students. The danger of this method is that it borders on a feeling among thè students that the teacher has abducted his/her role.

At the other end, in a completely directive method, the teacher is in complete command of the class, and leads and conducts the class as he/she thinks fit; the case method almost turns into a lecture with minimal participation from the students; and sometimes the students are even discouraged from interjecting questions.

The teacher should partially direct the discussion without taking full control of the teaching task. The teacher should remain in front and

- Create the right atmosphere to get student co-operation and positive participation.
- Create proper learning environment.
- Convince the class that the skills developed through case discussion are important to their professional growth.
- Facilitate the discussion and encourage widespread participation.
- Ask leading and searching questions.
- Increase class understanding of the complexities of the case by providing information when needed.
- Motivate non-participants; encourage shy students.
- Control overly aggressive students and provide conceptual/learning inputs arising from the case.
- Synthesize and summarise the discussion at the end.
- Give feedback to the class about the individual and group performance.

The teacher should present his own analysis after the students have exhausted all the arguments and no more positive contribution is likely to come from them and/or have missed some significant points. The teacher should not give the class an impression that his/her analysis and solution are the best but discuss whether the situation was handled properly or not. Students may be interested to know what happened afterwards.

Conducting a Case Class

Extreme care is necessary to identify cases, which relate to the subject matter being covered and the level of understanding and exposure to the case study method of the participants. For a suitable way of teaching approach the teacher has to decide a. how he/she will get the student involvement, b. whether the session will be structured or unstructured, c. how you will start the class; what opening remarks you will make and generate discussion, d. remember that he/she plays effectively the role of a leader, coach, teacher, timekeeper, synthesizer and summarizer.

The teacher has to create a proper learning climate to elicit co-operation and positive participation from the students. The class should be told what they have to gain from the case method (like development of analytical, problem-solving and communication skills). The teacher needs to take a positive classroom leadership role. This means the teacher should have complete command over the facts as given in the case; students should not be afraid of making mistakes and the teacher should not dominate the discussion nor convert the question-answer session into a lecture.

Feedback, both positive as well as negative, is a great motivating factor for the students. Students should be told in advance, how they will be evaluated and later on, about the method of assessment of their performance.

Teaching Suggestions

Students should be informed well in advance, the policy on who has to make a presentation and when. A 'lecturette' may be given if concepts and techniques are to be introduced in addition to circulation of technical note and/or an auxiliary note in advance; short time of in the middle of a case is needed to clarify/amplify concepts.

A teacher should ask probing questions that force the students to expand their arguments; use more neutral rather than antagonistic words, to encourage them to think clearly. It may be necessary to rephrase what the student said, to see if the meaning is clear to all concerned or to assist the student to express his/her thought clearly. Students should be given every opportunity in class to demonstrate their degree of preparation prior to the class and provide evaluative feedback in words and actions. Further, when you find the class is fatigued or bogged down by the complexity of the case, take off should be taken to summarize the discussion so far, either by the teacher or by the students themselves.

In a concluding session initial disjointed odds and ends should ultimately be tied to common theme. You should summarize and reinforce important issues arising out of the case. In wrapping up the case discussion the teacher can give some conceptual inputs that will tie experience to theory.

Case Method of Learning

The case study requires students to do most of their studying before the class, as contrasted with the lecture method, in which most of the study occurs later, as class notes are reviewed. It requires the student to prepare well in advance so as to be able to give a good presentation in the class, to understand and appreciate fully the arguments and presentations of other fellow students in class and effectively take part in the classroom discussion. The student has to place himself/herself in the role of the Manager and make decision and plan the action necessary based on the facts of the case and as he/she interprets them.

The student should not doubt the factual information given in the case; it has to be accepted as true; but they have to read between the lines to draw significant conclusions. The case may also give opinions of case characters and their subjective interpretations of events. These, however, can be doubted and challenged and a different opinion formed, if found more convincing. Students have to accept the financial data collected by the case writer, they can interpret it as he/she deems fit, considering the assumptions used.

Steps in the Case Study - Problem Solving Format

Student should read the case carefully, but very quickly, once, to make himself/herself familiar with the topic, the case characters, the leading actor whose role you are likely to play, the general nature and quality of the evidence given, and some idea of the problem(s) to be solved.

Student should read the case thoroughly a second time, at a much slower and thoughtful rate. Should take notes of important facts and assimilate the data provided. From this second reading a student should be able to abstract 1.a statement of the problem(s) involved, 2. the nature of the decision(s) facing the manager and 3.constraints opportunities and resources, which influence the actions, the manager can take.

Student should prepare analysis and recommendations, using either a general-purpose problem solving format (discussed below) or some specific analytical technique that you think will help.

The main steps in general purpose problem-solving format are as follows:

- Analyse the present situation.
- Forecast the future situation. This helps in indentifying the future constraints and opportunities affecting the outcomes of the planned actions.
- Identify the problem(s) or areas for improvement. Make a problem statement in terms that allows for later measurements of how well the problem has been solved.
- Set objectives or goals for achievement.
- Identify possible alternative courses of actions and predict their outcomes or consequences. In predicting the outcomes, a question of handling uncertainty may occur and techniques decision-making under uncertainty and risk may be necessary.
- Choose the alternatives / take a decision.

Writing a Case-Analysis Paper

It is important to cover 'what you recommend and why you recommend it' in case analysis paper. A student has to follow the teacher's instructions in writing a case analysis paper.

Following guidelines are useful in writing an analysis paper:

- Prepare a summary report of what you recommend and why you recommend it. You should add a summary page to every report as it makes a brief quick important reading.
- You should state the important facts and relevant data about the present position and forecast if necessary.

- Identify the main problem areas given in the case.
- List out alternative actions that might be taken, with predicted consequences of each alternative.
- Describe in detail of the recommended action and its consequences.
- The appraisal of the case should be thorough and effective.

There are two main ways of conducting a case-class discussion either an individual or a group responsibility. In the first situation each student prepares the case-analysis without any pre-class discussion with other students. The class consists of presentations of one student's viewpoint after another. This procedure tends to be boring as no fresh grounds are covered after a few initial presentations and lacks opportunity to discuss any points on which differences that might occur. Another variation of this method is that the students do not make complete presentations but the teacher asks a few students to put forward their viewpoints on different aspects of the case. This approach of building a case analysis bit by bit from selected inputs from each student adds breadth and emphasizes the wide variety of ideas that can be identified in the case material. This can however, be slow and result in loss of interest of all students.

The other approach consists of Group analysis, the pre-class discussion groups will reach a consensus within each group and nominate a spokesperson to present that viewpoint in the class. This allows more time for class discussion as it reduces time due to individual presentations. The teacher may set up role playing exercise where one group makes a formal presentation and the other groups take the role of a critical audience, putting forward questions or counter arguments. This method is akin to a presentation made by a manager to a group of senior managers.

In summary, it is essential to ensure that the case method is an integral part of the programme (subject, module) for which it is being used. When properly used, it provides one of the best learning methods as it stimulates independent thinking, self discovery and learning from peers. However, due care should be given to the suitability of the cohort size and the adequacy of the facilities available for conducting the analysis. The timing for the use of the case study depends on the topic which the case deals with and its place within the module syllabus.

CASE 1

INFORMATION AND LIBRARY SERVICES – A PROBLEM OF RESOURCE ALLOCATION

Dr B A Chansarkar
Middlesex University Business School, London (UK)

Abstract

This case pertains to service provision and associated issues of Information and Library Services (ILS) of a well established Institute of Management (Kalpana Institute of Management KIM). Information about books issued and returned is recorded on a regular basis in ILS. The observed patterns of service provision are used in reallocating of resources so as to overcome the dissatisfaction with the service provision in the library. There is concern the way the situation about dissatisfaction with the service provision was handled in KIM. Additional information about time tabling of classes is now being synchronised so as to ease the pressure on staff time for dealing the demand of services in ILS.

The Information and Library Services

The Information and Library Services (ILS) of a well established Institute of Management (Kalpana Institute of Management KIM) constitutes a true learning centre. It operates as an open access system and is open to users for book issuing between 08.00 to 22.00 hour's everyday of the week. To facilitate self-learning among the students, the Library is kept open 24 hours a day round the year, barring public holidays. The ILS is located in a specially designed building adjacent to the Institute's 'main campus. The ILS has well-established linkages with the libraries in other institutions and corporate training centres. It has a high degree of computerisation for providing high quality service and fast transactions. The ILS is currently managed by a Librarian who is ably supported by four Assistant Librarians, each dealing with responsibilities for different services offered by the ILS. Three Library clerks/assistants work with each of the Assistant Librarian. The ILS has five peons/library attendants to help on overall management of the ILS. The ogranisational structure of the ILS is shown in Figure 1 attached.

Figure 1: Organisational Structure of the ILS

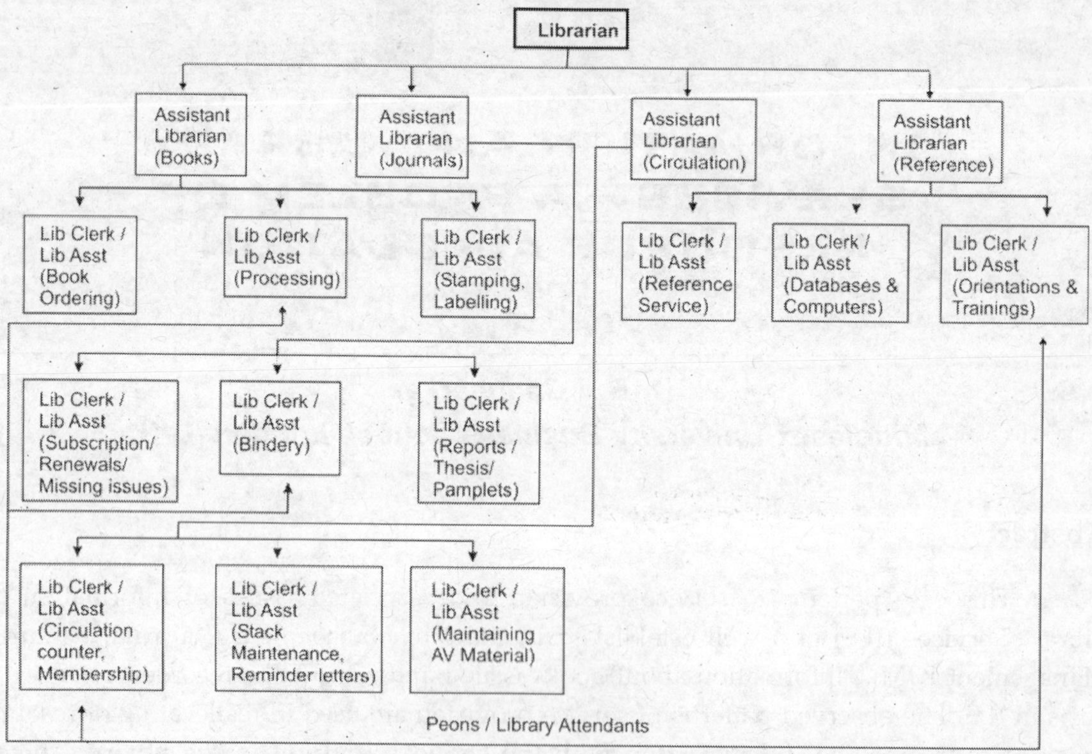

The Resources of the ILS

The library has an extensive collection of books (over 46,000) covering all aspects of business, management and also related subjects such as economics, behavioral sciences, information technology, law, quantitative methods etc. The periodical section is a vital source for academic research and up-to-date business information. The ILS has an extensive collection of journals and periodicals of both Indian and foreign origin. In addition, it holds annual reports and in the last few years electronic journals too. There are over 4,500 videocassettes, 3,200 audio cassettes, in addition to the VCRs and CDs which are available for reference and short loans. Like most library services, the ILS operates a shift system for its staff. There are three main shifts currently operating 07.30 to 15.00 hours; 12.30 to 20.00 hours and 14.30 to 22.30 hours. A quarter of the library assistants and attendants work in a middle shift 12.30 to 20.00 hours. This middle shift acts as a buffer for reallocating staff when someone avails his/her leave and away from work. The ILS, as far as possible, tries to avoid using over time to staff to accommodate leave and contingencies. The ILS management is guided by a 'Library Committee', which is responsible for providing the resources and is headed by the Pro vice-chancellor (VC) Professor Mukund Patel. The Committee has representation from all departments, management (pro-VC, ex-officio member) and the Students Union. The Committee monitors the working of the ILS and deals with any complaints against the ILS. It also conducts survey annually to gauge the usage of the ILS services and is responsible for the implementation of the suggestions received from the survey. The 'Library Committee' meets once a semester. The Committee has a significant role in the purchase of books, selection of appropriate journals and also appointment of staff for the ILS.

Service Provision of the ILS

The Librarian, Dr John Abrahams, is quite satisfied with the efficient service the ILS provides. Most of the ILS staff time is spent on issuing books and collecting the returned books. Reminders are sent out regularly informing the borrowers about the forthcoming date of return, as ILS imposes nominal penalty for late returns. John has encountered difficulty in ensuring timely returns of books and especially journals borrowed by the Faculty. The ILS also carries out stock verification for 15 days annually when the Library is closed completely except for acceptance of returned books. During this period of stock verification the ILS also tries to complete binding, weeding and labeling of books. Periodicals, cassettes and CDs are issued for a limited period of six hours. This has improved recently when the ILS introduced a strict and severe penalty system for late returns. In some instances, no further book etc is issued to the defaulting borrower. The ILS provides inter-library loan facility and other services such as E-Resources (Integrated Management System, Capitaline 2000), Trend Analysis (Financial package), CME (Centre for Monitoring Indian Economy), Elsevier, EBSCO (on-line journal database) and ECCH (European Case Clearing House). The ILS provides the Faculty, facilities for research through Contents page of new journals and 'What is New?' series.

Demand for Services

The ILS regularly monitors the service provision. The pattern of books issued and returned during the week is shown in Figure 2. The hourly pattern of books issued and returned during the day of week is shown in Figure 3.

Figure 2: Weekly pattern of number of Books issued and returned

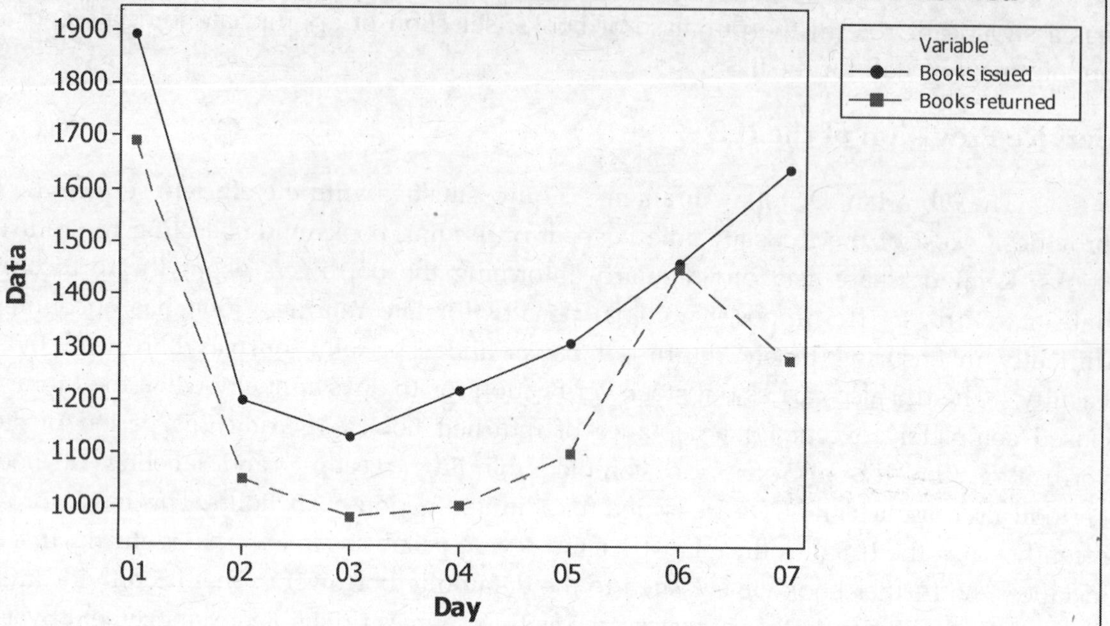

01=Monday , 02=Tuesday .... 07=Sunday

The demand for services, in addition, fluctuates with the deadline for coursework, assignments and prior to the examinations. Mr. Vasant Desai, the President of the Students Union (also member of the Library Committee) met the Pro vice-chancellor, Professor Mukund Patel (who is the ex-officio Chairperson of the Library Committee), at an informal gathering. During the conversation, Vasant informed Prof. Patel about the complaints he had heard from some students. There were severe delays in service provision in the library during certain hours of the day and great difficulty in getting journals and reference materials. Vasant also casually mentioned that this could lead to student unrest if the service provision did not improve soon. Professor Patel who chairs the Library Committee immediately on arrival in his office, directs the Librarian Mr. John Abrahams to investigate the matter and submit plan for improving the service provision to avoid anticipated student unrest. John is disturbed and unhappy to have been instructed to deal with the matter without any prior consultation or discussion with him or the Committee. He, however, reluctantly investigates the daily routine work schedule of the ILS. The daily issues and returns of the books recorded at two hourly intervals (e.g., upto 10.00am, 10.00 to noon, …etc) for each day of the week (Figure 3) are the outcome of this investigation.

Sheila, Assistant Librarian (Books) discusses with John the peak times for servicing the Library. She suggests that the partial solution may lie in re-scheduling classes so that students have dispersed free time to use the ILS. This is expected to improve the efficiency of the service as students will come to the Library in their free time at different intervals than what it is now and will not require extra resources. As a result, John requests the timetable coordinator to supply him the schedule of the current timetable so as to ascertain the relationship of demand for the ILS services with the lecture/seminar schedule.

Figure 3: Number of Books issued and returned

Each day of the week at 2 hourly intervals

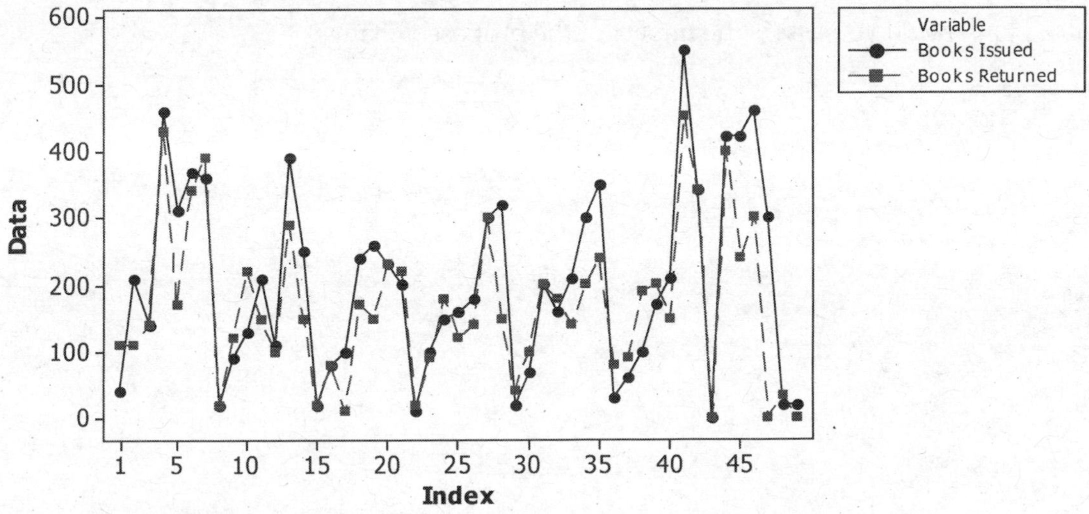

01=Monday upto 10am, 02=Monday 10am to noon .... 07=Monday 8 to 10 pm
1 to 7 =Monday, 8 to 14=Tuesday.............. 43 to 49=Sunday

The Outcome

- It was agreed that all complaints about the ILS be channeled through the 'Library Committee'.
- To avoid excessive demand for the ILS services, a re-scheduling of full-time classes was implemented.
- A box for dropping returned books was put outside the ILS for students to drop books outside the working hours, thus reducing the demand on staff time.
- Re-allocation of library assistants and clerks was done, increasing the numbers during the peak demand and reducing the staff during the lean hours.
- Stringent rules and heavy penalty fines for late returns were introduced to ensure that the Faculty and students returned the books and journals in time.

Questions:

1. Comment on the way John Abrahams handled the situation; especially being asked without prior consultation to investigate the compliant lodged verbally.
2. Critically evaluate the information collected by the ILS to resolve the situation. What additional information is required to resolve such a situation?
3. How would you assess the impact of the proposed changes?

CASE 2

DEMAND FORECASTING

Dr B A Chansarkar
Middlesex University Business School, London (UK).

Abstract

"Phatak's Ice cream" is a well-established company currently holding 15 per cent of the ice cream market in India. The company manufactures and supplies ice cream and other cold drinks. The company estimates, according to the calculations of Dr Kulkarni, the Marketing Director, sales per shop to be Rupees 14,000 per shop over the nest year. Reena, newly appointed Marketing Manager, proposes that the company should franchise in New Delhi and estimates that using the sales per shop, assuming the present trend to continue, to contribute Rupees 5,152,000. She strongly advocates to enter the franchise. This has created the dilemma for company whether to enter the new franchise or to continue as before. The case analysis should help in understanding which forecasting method is appropriate in such situation and thus help the company in taking appropriate action.

Background Information

"Phatak's Ice cream" is a well-established company currently holding 15 per cent of the ice cream market in India. The company manufactures and supplies ice cream and other cold drinks. Nearly 80 per cent of its trade is in ice cream market. The head office of the company is based in Pune and the company over the period of last 22 years has a sizeable number of shops (509 at the last count) spread over different cities of Maharashtra State and neighboring States of Gujarat and Madhya Pradesh.

"Phatak's Ice cream" was started by Mr. Shyam Phatak in Pune in the year 1987. In the year 1990 two of his sons joined the business, by which time the Company had 20 outlets throughout Pune and also a franchise with three outlets in Mumbai. The Company had acquired a chain of shops at the end of the year 1996 in Ahmedabad district in Gujarat and another similar chain of shops at the end of the year 1999 in Jabalpur district of Madhya Pradesh. The ice cream and soft drinks industry in the year 1996 of company's trading, has seen a shift in the market due to introduction of deep freezers which has increased sales for home consumption. In the year 2002 'Phatak's Ice cream' introduced soft scoope light ice cream. This new product can be used straight from the freezer and this has increased sales and the trend is likely to continue.

'Phatak's Ice cream' is famous for its quality production and is known to be a leader in the industry. It has introduced over the years ice creams of different flavours and other companies follow the trend established by 'Phatak's Ice cream'. Families with children are the main customers of the Company. Cities make up majority of the market and in small rural area 'Phatak's Ice cream' has successfully franchised its trade.

Mr. Shyam Phatak, the Managing Director of the Company has asked the Marketing Director Dr. Sunil Kulkarni to estimate the sales of the Company for the next year. Miss Reena Sethi has recently joined the Company as Marketing Manager from a leisure company where she was manager of a restaurant for seven years. She tells Dr. Kulkarni that based on her experience and knowledge of the market in North of India, the Company should expand in that market - initially in New Delhi. She advocates franchising to a small company called 'Ice Cream Parlow', which has 40 shops. Sunil is opposed to the idea of franchising in New Delhi and asks Reena to conduct marketing research first to study the demand for 'Phatak's Ice cream' in New Delhi. Sunil tells Reena that his research indicates that the demand for ice cream is seasonal and sales peak during the summer months and also during the marriage seasons. He estimates, using simple linear regression over the last six years information (Table 1), Y (Sales) = -64.07 + 1.40X (Number of shops), the sales of ice cream for the next year 2007, to be Rupees 65,000,000.

Sales of 'Phatak's Ice cream'

The sales of 'Phatak's Ice cream' since the beginning of trading in Maharashtra were as follows:

Table (1): Sales of 'Phatak's Ice cream' ('000 Rupees)

Year	Number of shops	Sales ('000 Rupees)
1985	1	25
1986	4	69
1987	7	300
1988	10	650
1989	20	1,200
1990	32	1,900
1991	47	2,810
1992	60	3,720
1993	70	4,240
1994	110	6,380
1995	132	9,000
1996	154	11,650
1997	170	14,300
1998	190	18,600
1999	221	23,100
2000	236	27,700
2001	289	33,500
2002	328	39,300
2003	360	44,100
2004	400	49,900
2005	446	55,700
2006	509	64,300

Source: The Company Records. (November 2006).

Reena's Analysis

Reena conducts a preliminary analysis of the sales of the Company. Graph 1 below shows the growth of shops of 'Phatak's Ice cream' and Graph 2 the pattern of sales in relation to time.

Graph 1 'Phatak's Ice cream' shops

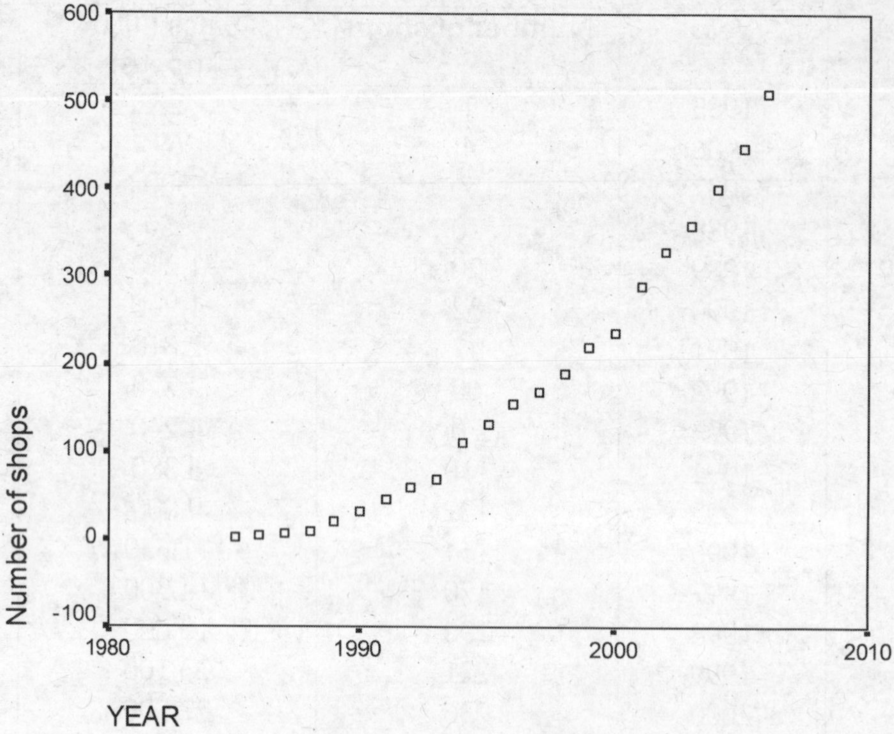

Graph 2 Sales of 'Phatak's Ice cream' ('000 Rupees)

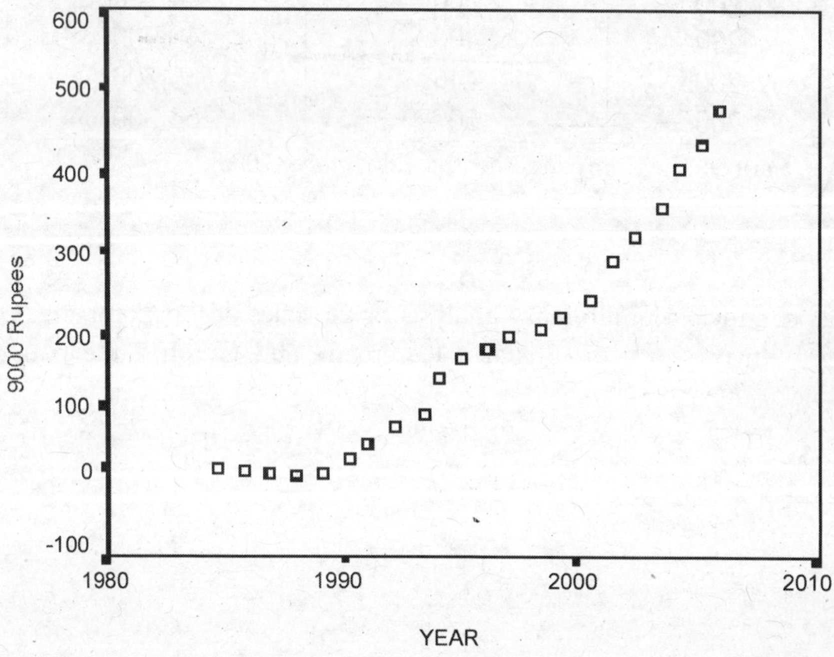

Reena observes that the growth is non-linear and however, the patterns growth of shops and sales follow the same. She, therefore, decides to calculate the sales per outlet and the outcome is shown below in Table (2) and Graph 3:

Table (2): Sales per shop of 'Phatak's Ice cream' ('000 Rupees)

Year	Sales per shop ('000 Rupees)
1985	25.00
1986	17.25
1987	42.85
1988	65.00
1989	60.00
1990	59.38
1991	59.79
1992	62.00
1993	60.57
1994	58.00
1995	68.18
1996	75.65
1997	84.12
1998	97.90
1999	104.52
2000	117.37
2001	115.92
2002	119.82
2003	122.50
2004	124.75
2005	124.89
2006	126.33

Graph 3 Sales per shop ('000 Rupees)

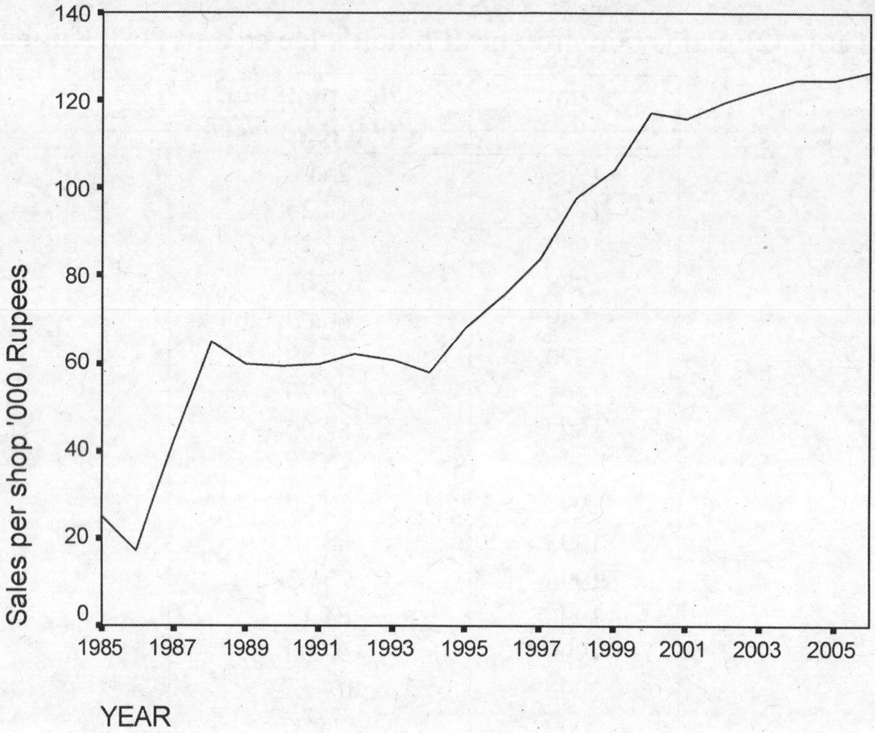

The sales per shop have mostly stabilised over the last six years and using this information she calculates the growth pattern of sales per shop using the last seven years data., Sales per shop = 114.55 + 1.78 X (Time). Using this the estimated sales for the year 2007 to be Rupees 65,690,000. She further states that if 40 new outlets were to become part of the Phatak's ice cream and the present trend continued, then the sales would increase by nearly Rupees 5,152,000. She therefore, strongly recommends that Phatak should go ahead with franchise.

Questions:

1. Comment on the method adopted by Dr Kulkarni and the estimates of the sales so generated.
2. Comment on the method adopted by Reena in estimating the sales for the year 2007 and the recommendation she makes.
3. Should Dr Kulkarni agree to the proposal by Reena in franchising in New Delhi?
4. What additional information is necessary to make a meaningful recommendation?

CASE 3

THE INDIAN AVIATION SECTOR

Dr S Mishra
New Delhi Institute of Management
New Delhi, india

Abstract

India's civil aviation sector has been witnessing a plethora of changes over the last few years owing to the government's favourable initiatives. With the aviation boom, one can examine inevitable changes in domestic and international markets. The growth of new low cost private players in domestic market, permission to domestic airlines to fly international destinations and competition among international players (using Indian air space) for market share in overseas market are some of the issues which are affecting the two Indian state-owned players, Indian Airlines (IA) and Air India (AI). As a result, the state-owned players are facing an obvious decline in their market shares coupled with some specific problems, which have been duly mentioned throughout this case. The sector is confronting a number of problems viz. shortage of key airports, lack of infrastructure facilities and nonetheless, the dearth of skills-specific manpower. Besides presenting an actionable understanding of the Indian aviation Industry, this case study also makes an effort to comprehend the competitive dynamics prevalent thereof. It also necessarily shifts the focus of these two state-owned players from being merely on price cut measures to redefining their respective marketing strategies for culminating the much sought after brand image.

Introduction

Mr. Thulasidas, the Managing Director of Air India looked at the report in front of him. It was titled "The Changing Face of Indian Aviation Industry' and it had been prepared by a reputed market research firm at the instance of civil aviation ministry. Mr. Thulasidas, after going through the report called Ms. Sushma Chawla, the chairperson and MD of Indian Airlines and after thorough conversation they decided to call a meeting of senior officials of

Air-India (AI), Indian Airlines (IA) and also representatives of the civil aviation ministry. The very next day, Mr. Thulasidas started the meeting by giving a brief description of the report to the members.

Mr. Thulasidas: Good morning to all of you! Today's meeting has been called to make you aware certain prominent facts regarding our airlines. At present, AI has a fleet of 39 aircrafts and operates on long-haul routes like the US and Europe while IA operates with 63 aircrafts and it's core strength is its nationwide connectivity. Well, if we look the records for the past few years, Air India has been steadily losing market share to international airlines like British Airways, KLM, Emirates and Singapore Airlines. Despite being the national carrier, AI's market share of outbound traffic from India has come down to just 20 per cent from 40 per cent in the 1970s. Besides this, Indian Airlines, which aims to join a global airline alliance in the long term, has also noticed a dip in market share in 2004-05.

Ms Sushma Chawla: Well, in addition to these fact mentioned by Mr. Thulasidas, the domestic aviation industry is also facing a number of problems spurred by the arrival of new start-ups with low fares. Another recent change is the permission of the more established private airlines to be allowed to fly overseas, the exception being that flights to the Gulf region will not be permitted for three years. It has brought Air-India in a direct face-off with domestic carriers in overseas market.

Mr Thulasidas: We have been witnessing this changing scenario since last few years and as a result we have given the task to a reputed research firm who has submitted a detailed report on Indian airlines industry. The emphasis is on the changes made in the aviation industry, the problems faced by players in general as well as specific problems faced by IA and AI. They have also suggested strategies to deal with this changing scenario. The report goes like this.........

Indian Airlines Industry – its background and overview

The history of Indian aviation industry dates back to the early 1930s, when one of the leading Indian business houses, the Tatas set up the Tata Airlines. There was limited activity in the field over the next two decades despite eight more private companies entered the fray. The government nationalised the airlines industry in 1953, with enactment of Air Corporation Act, and assets of nine existing air companies were transferred to the two new corporations – Air India International and the Indian Airlines. In 1962, Air India International was renamed Air India Ltd. A third government-owned airline, Vayudoot, was also a domestic carrier in the early 1990s. It provided feeder service between smaller cities and the larger places served by Air India and Indian Airlines. By 1994 Indian Airlines had taken over Vayudoot. Another publicly owned company, Pawan Hans, runs helicopter service, mostly to offshore locations and other areas that cannot be served by fixed-wing aircraft.

In 1986, private airlines were allowed to operate chartered and non-scheduled services under an 'Air Taxi' scheme. The scheme was introduced to boost tourism and augment domestic air services. The carriers were however, not allowed to publish time schedules or issue tickets to passengers. After 40 years, in 1994 Air Corporation Act was repealed, ending the monopoly of the national air corporations and thus enabling entry of private operators. The government approved eight private carriers to start domestic operations; these players were Jet Airways, Sahara, Indian International, Archana, East West, NEPC, Modiluft, and Damania. Although it has resulted competition from private airlines, but some of the airline operators disappeared without a trace.

The Air Corporations Act 1953 prohibited any person or company to operate any scheduled air transport services from, to or across India. Therefore, two corporations (i.e. AI and IA) enjoyed a monopoly status in the scheduled air transport services market. As a result, prior to 1992 while these two public sector airlines enjoyed a command in the domestic sector, today a dozen airlines are competing for a market share. During that era, the Indian public had to wait days to get reservations on Indian Airlines and Air India. The services were often shoddy, the tickets were expensive and connections inadequate. After 1992, there has been a marked change in the civil aviation scenery in India as the private operators changed the dynamics of the industry. Thus, India's two national carriers, which ruled the country's skies, found it difficult to retain their market share in competitive atmosphere. Indian Airlines that enjoyed a market share of 65 per cent in 1997-98, slid to 38 per cent in 2004-05. There were entries and exits in civil aviation industry, but Jet Airways and Air Sahara became the two leading private scheduled domestic air traffic operators, functioning as full-service airlines, which have given a tough competition to national carriers. They have showed passengers what the romance of flying was all about, by offering lower fares and new aircraft and providing better service. As a result, Air India and Indian Airlines realised the importance of marketing and public relations.

Although, there has been a dramatic rise in the levels of passenger and cargo traffic, from just 5.1 million passengers in 1970, domestic and international passenger traffic has grown to nearly 59 million passengers in 2004-05. Table 1 in Annexure shows the passenger and cargo traffic for the last four decades.

The recent growth in the Civil Aviation Sector has been more than encouraging. During the last ten years the growth in passenger traffic has been a spectacular 125 per cent. By 2010, the forecast is that air traffic will increase to around 90 million. Domestic and international passenger traffic in India is projected to grow annually at 12.5 per cent and 7 per cent over the next decade. Similarly, air cargo exports from India are expected to rise from the present 0.8 million tonnes to 2.4 million tonnes while domestic cargo will rise from 300,000 tonnes to over 1 million tonnes by 2010 Such growth is resultant of paradigm shift towards greater liberalization and significant private sector participation in infrastructure development. Liberalization of air services in the last one year has created history, which has resulted into increased connectivity and also helped in lowering fares. The current scenario in aviation industry has made these two state-owned players to understand and combat with other domestic and international players.

More Players in the Market

Players in the domestic market

Due to liberalized government policy in the aviation sector, the Indian budget airline industry is taking to the skies. Wallet-friendly aviation players are appearing, much to the delight of the Indian budget air traveller. At present, the sector is witnessing a flurry of activity:-five low cost warriors have already launched their flights and around 10 other players are planning to start operations. A brief description of these players is given below:

Air Deccan was the first airline, which brought the budget airline concept to the Indian skies. It has unleashed cut-throat competition in the aviation scene with fares mostly equaling similar to train fares. Air Deccan, which took off in August 2003, placed a massive 30-aircraft order with Airbus in 2004. It was the first private airline in India to fly an Airbus.

Kingfisher Airlines is a Value Carrier (i.e those who offer some frills despite low fare), which is promoted and financed by UB group Chairman Vijay Mallaya and was launched in May 2005. Kingfisher Airlines charges are higher than Air Deccan's, but substantially less than those of the big players. It emphasizes on spunky, well-done interiors and trained airhostesses. In November 2005, Kingfisher Airlines placed orders for 50 aircrafts, including 30 Airbus A320s and 20 ATR72-500s.

Royal Airways Spicejet (formerly Modi Luft) which is promoted by Malwood group controlled by London based Kansagra family, launched its operations in May 2005. SpiceJet, a budget airline, has five Boeings in its fold and has placed orders for 10 more.

Go Air, promoted by the Wadia Group , was launched in November 2005 and operates flights to more than 10 major cities in India. Go Air's fleet consists of three Airbus A320-200 aircraft. The airline has signed a MOU for 10 Airbus A320's with an option for a further 10 A320's.

Another entrant to an increasingly competitive scenario is Paramount Airways, a Tamil Nadu-based company that began operations in October 2005. Paramount has leased five Embraer 170s and three Embraer 175s and placed orders for five more. It is the only airline in India to fly the Embraer. It has also ordered 10 Boeing 787s.

In addition, there are few more new startup airlines, which have no flight operations currently.

IndiGo Airlines, promoted by a travel and technology group Inter globe with a turnover close to Rs 2000 crores and is headed by Rahul Bhatia. It has placed an order for 100 Airbus A320 aircraft and plans to launch services in July/August 2006, once it receives the first brand new Airbus A320 aircraft. IndiGo plans to induct six aircrafts by December 2006 and another nine in 2007.

Indus Airways, low-cost but all-frills carrier, had its first Operations as Northern Airways, before Independence. It seeks to restore the proud heritage of Northern Airways by inducting state-of-the-art aircrafts and offering services, which would have made

Northern Airways proud. Indus Airways will start its services with the ultra modern, Canadian made, CRJ-200 jetliner. It hopes to launch services from mid 2006 with five leased 50-seater Embraer RJ-145 aircraft.

Air one, the Bangalore based airline plans to operate 50-seat Embraer ERJ-145 regional jet aircraft with a base in Bangalore. The airline will commence flight operations in 2006.

Premier airway, a Chennai-based low-cost carrier, plans to commence operations by the end of year 2006.

Air Dravida, the Chennai-based airline plans to operate Bombardier CRJ-200 aircraft and launch operations by June 2006.

City Air, with operational headquarters at Chennai and promoted by a Dubai-based NRI ,plans to launch flights with Airbus A320 aircraft in early 2006.

Eastwest Airlines (which took wings in the early 90s, folded up in 1998) is also expected to make a comeback this year. Its promoters now plan to re-launch the airline in a low-cost format.

Kerala Airlines plans to operate from Cochin International Airport to various Gulf destinations. The airline, if and when it takes off, would be the first state government controlled airline in India.

With the entry of low cost airlines, the market shares of established full-service carriers have dropped over the last one-year. Even though the air travel market is growing at a rapid pace, the low cost carriers are cornering a significant part of the growth. This is clear from a comparison of current market shares of various domestic carriers with last year figures, depicted in Table 2 in Annexure.

The low cost airlines would continue to grow as they are addressing a different segment of the market. They would continue to gain market share at a rapid pace as more and more travellers take to the skies.

Another trigger point in the fast growing domestic aviation sector is the acquisition of Air Sahara by Jet Airways in January 2006, which has concluded a major consolidation. This would give Jet a significant lead over second placed Indian Airlines. Jet Airways has been one of the biggest corporate success stories of the '90s, emerging as the largest domestic carrier while maintaining service standards comparable to premium international airlines. After the merger, the combined market share of Jet-Sahara would be close to 45 per cent even after a possible rationalisation of routes.

Players (domestic and international) affecting overseas markets

As a result of open sky policy, India has allowed domestic commercial airlines to fly long haul international routes; a move it hopes will stoke competition and drive down prices. However, only state-owned carriers will be able to fly the lucrative Gulf routes, to countries such as Kuwait and Saudi Arabia, for at least three years. Jet Airways and Air Sahara are the two companies, which will have the benefit initially. On one hand; foreign carriers are being allowed to fly into India, (for instance the government has given out 47,000 seats a week during the last three years to foreign airlines) and at another level the number of seats given away to foreign carriers in the south east Asia has more than doubled in three years i.e., from 14,000 to as much as 32,000 seats a week currently. The government has also agreed on a policy with South East Asian countries, under which their carriers can now fly daily to the four metros without any reciprocal rights for Indian carriers.

India is seen as the world's second largest growing economy after China and so airlines of all countries have now focused their attention on the Indian travel market. Be it British, American or Asian carriers, all want to fly into India to cash in the situation, and each one is offering the most competitive fares. At present, 51 foreign airlines fly into India, which carry 70% of two-way traffic.

Besides this, foreign airlines are getting more slots at Indian airports now.A recent bilateral air services agreement between India and the United Kingdom opened the gates for increase in destination and frequency numbers, and British Airways seems to make best use of this long-awaited opportunity.

Another path breaking agreement, which has opened a new era in civil aviation partnership, is Open Skies Air Transport Agreement between India and US. This agreement has replaced the 1956 agreement, which had restricted the airlines' choices on the number of flights, the cities that could be served and the prices charged. Now the airlines of both countries can utilise an additional half-a-million seats every year.

With air connectivity between India and the rest of the world growing, competition on most international routes have also increased. Airlines are using the low fare bait to win customers. In spite of rising fuel prices and tight profit margins, several international airlines operating out of India have further dropped fares to access a larger market. Thai Airways, Malaysian Airlines and Austrian Airways are some of the leading players among others.

Besides this, the proposed unified aviation pact between India and the European Union (EU) may trigger a major fare war in the India-Europe airline sector. Although, the air fares to European destinations are already low but with skies opening up eventually, fares are expected to come down by another 20-25%.

Problems in Aviation Industry

Some of the problems in India's aviation industry that could create trouble are:

General Management (Infrastructural) Problems

Shortage of key airports: At present there are only six key airports - Mumbai, Delhi, Kolkata, Chennai, Bangalore and Hyderabad - which handle 80 percent of the civil aviation traffic on a daily basis. But these airports are filled and there is no space for additional aircraft. Moreover, development of airports in India has not kept pace with the mushrooming of airlines in the country. The up-gradation of international airports is also taking a long time. Recently, Andhra Pradesh announced six new airports in the state which include popular pilgrim destinations like Tirupati and Puttaparthi. (Mumbai Mirror, 19th January 2007). In addition, a much needed renovation and expansion of the fast growing Vizag city is to be taken up. Both Kingfisher Airlines and Air Deccan are planning to start operations there.

Lack of infrastructure facilities at airports: The increase in passenger traffic calls for upgraded infrastructure facilities. Some of the key issues of development of airports are inadequacy of space and congestion at emigration clearance.

Besides this, congestion at airports also leads to increase flying time. There are more planes waiting to land at Delhi (especially in winter due to foggy weather) than the airport infrastructure can cope with. As a result, the planes are made to circle in the sky before they can be given the permission to land. This wait in the skies can often be as long as 30 minutes. For every extra minute an airline has to keep its planes flying as a result of this congestion, it incurs an additional fuel cost Rs 6,000 per aircraft. This is a huge additional cost for airlines already hit hard by the steady increase of aviation turbine fuel prices.

In addition, development of airport infrastructure is necessary, as airports all over the world are not mere stopover points but destinations by themselves. They are well equipped with amenities like shopping malls, restaurants, health clubs, internet facilities, rest rooms and what not. Indian Airports need such type of developments to become compatible to global trends.

In this context it is interesting to note that 'non-aeronautical revenues are set to bloat the purses of airports being developed by the private sector' (P R Sanjai, Business Standard, Times of India, 10th January, 2007). An average 50:50 mix is targeted by both the private and government operated airports.

Lack of maintenance facility at airport: Indian airports are very poor on maintenance facilities at airports. Private airlines are not allowed to establish hangars for major maintenance overhauls at airports and consequently have to outsource maintenance activity to high cost locations abroad. European aircraft maker Airbus Industries is in talk with the sate-owned Hindustan Aeronautics to set up a maintenance, repair and overhaul facilities for aircraft airframes in the country, mostly likely in Bangalore. Airports of Authority of India (at Hyderabad), Wadia family launching the GoAir with Singapore Airlines and Essar group are also in discussion to set up other centres. However, the need of the hour is to establish maintenance and engineering departments at the airport premises.

Finance Problems

Increase in expenses due to rise in ATF (aviation turbine fuel) prices: When it comes to pricing of air passenger and cargo traffic the main problem is high cost of aviation turbine fuel and high tax that is paid as compared to foreign airlines. ATF comprises 25 per cent of the operational cost of airlines. Currently the high cost of Aviation Turbine Fuel is compelling the airliners to levy a surcharge on fuel.

High landing and airport charges: Airport charges (comprising of landing charges, routine navigation facility charges and terminal navigation landing charges) in India are estimated to be 78 per cent higher than the global average. The 12 international airports of India levy charges up to 20 per cent higher than others.

HR Problem

Problem of staff shortage: Currently with the aviation boom, India is facing dearth of skill specific manpower; the problem is not only for trained pilots but also aeronautical engineers and air traffic controllers in an expanding aviation market. This has resulted in higher responsibility jobs being done by less experienced professionals increasing the fear of accidents that can bring the aviation sector growth back to square one. Airlines have started recruiting foreign pilots to overcome the shortages. It may be India will have more foreign pilots than Indian pilots. However, hiring foreign pilots has its problems. Some pilots have communication problems due to lack of comprehension of English, week-long leave, and payment of tax bills. This requires adequate training facilities for pilots and engineers.

Operational Problems

Problem of catering short haul routes connectivity: It should be noted that in the last decade a large number of private airlines had entered the domestic market but, barring a few, all have had to exit the market especially those catering to the short haul route. India needs to strengthen these routes to promote connectivity between Districts, Divisions and States. It also needs to promote these routes for Business Development, trade and tourism. To do this the economics of Airline Operations should be rationally examined and corrective measures taken to help the industry.

Problems Specific to IA and AI

Some of the problems faced by these two players are:

Marketing Problem

Intense competition by domestic and international players: Indian aviation business, which took wings in the year gone by, continues to grow by leaps and bounds. More airlines launch flights, domestic as well as international players, which are giving a tough fight to IA and AI. In domestic market, five new players have already started their operations while a large number of other players are expected to afloat by the end of 2006. In addition, low-fare airlines from the Gulf (Air Arabia) and South-east Asia (Air Asia and Tiger Airways), are also eyeing the Indian market.

At present, IA and AI are facing severe competition, under a revised air services agreement with USA. Both sides can designate any number of services to any point in the territory of the other country with full intermediate and beyond traffic rights. Similarly traffic rights were enhanced with 18 other countries also in order to enable greater connectivity to/from India e.g., Australia, UK, Germany, China, France, Netherlands,

Belgium, Canada, Singapore, Mauritius, New Zealand, UAE etc. This will lead to more flights and better connectivity from these countries to India providing more commercial opportunity to all operating carriers.

HR Problems

Huge staff strength: Another major issue, which requires serious attention is massive staff strength of AI and IA. Air India, employs 16,000-18,000 staff while Indian Airlines has staff strength of 20,000, much higher in terms of passenger route kilometres compared to international benchmarks. The employee-aircraft ratio of the Indian airlines is about 361:1, against the industry average of 200-250:1. For Jet Airways it is 173:1 and for American Airlines 128:1.

Poaching of manpower: Due to appearance of new players and resulting competition, there is a crippling shortage of pilots, commandants, ground staff and cabin crew for every airline. This results into poaching of trained staff by the private operators from these two low-paid state-owned airlines. The demand for pilots will exceed supply in the coming years as a result it will lead to higher costs for incumbents.

Finance Problem

Problem of higher expenses: These two state-owned players are plagued by problem of higher expenses due to maintenance and overhauling, and the direct result of an aged fleet. The average age of AI's and IA's fleet is about 17 years as compared to an age of 6-7 years internationally. This indicates the need for employing newer aircraft, which will help in not just cutting down the operating expenses, but also in building a much needed positive image of the airline on safety ground. Indian Airlines needs to bring its expenses down by rationalising the size, quality and mix of its fleet.

General Management Problem

Controlling in the hands of political leaders: Over the years, the working of these two players has been under political patronage, which adversely affected the viability of these players, and it has exacerbated distortions, inefficiencies and constraints for them. Despite the competitive environment faced by AI & IA, the government has barely allowed the managements of Air India and Indian Airlines to make any important decisions. Political leaders still control critical issues, which are required due to growing market, entry of new players and ageing of fleet, like appointing managers, deploying aircraft, deciding routes, fleet expansion etc.

Thulasidas's Concerns

As Mr. Thulasidas opened the last part of the report, he began to wonder that despite the actions taken by IA and AI in past, the prevailing situation in aviation industry has thrown formidable challenges for them; therefore they should focus not only on flexible market-driven fares but also on other areas.

Actions/ strategies of state-owned carriers in the past

- Focus on reduced pricing
- As the budget carrier battle hots up, country's flag carrier Air-India has set up a subsidiary called Air India Express, which is an international low-cost airline. Air India Express offers fares that are 25 per cent cheaper than the previous fares of AI.
- Cutting costs (through retirement schemes, rationalizing menus and better inventory control) without compromising on safety and the product,
- Investments in improving the ground support facilities and focusing on aggressive growth in fleet and up gradation of the existing aircraft.
- To compete both locally and globally, the Government has announced the 43-Airbus aircraft acquisition proposal of Indian Airlines and the 68 Boeing aircraft deal for Air India.
- The state-owned airlines, however, were not the only ones that went in for fleet expansion during the year. All the new entrants are also going for huge aircraft acquisition plans. Refer Table 3 for future acquisition plan of various players.
- Increasing the use of capacity, and customer base and also expanding flights substantially to major destinations. These players are also planning to improve tie-ups with selected international carriers so as to invade the local overseas market.
- Air India has started flights to Shanghai and Los Angeles and also introduced terminator flights from Ahmedabad to London. Air India has identified need for non-stop operations to USA and is tailoring its fleet acquisition accordingly. Services to the 12 new destinations have been planned in a phased manner.
- Offering excellent customer service and keeping up with the need of customers, by acquiring modern generation aircrafts with all the frills to attract the upper end market.

  Indian Airlines is focusing on new brands and logo, by dropping 'Airlines', (now known as 'Indian') the company wants to give more stress on the Indianness of the carrier. The change is also in a bid to attract younger people who are growing in the number of air passengers. Although, the brand and the name will be new, the company's name continues to be Indian Airlines Limited. With a view to enhance passenger appeal, Air India has undertaken major cabin interior refurbishment.

- Utilising IT

  These state-owned carriers besides hosting websites for online access have also introduced computerized check-in and an advance seat reservation facility. In 2004, IA introduced 'Netravel', an e-ticketing process for online booking. While in 2005, it also started mobile air ticket booking in India in collaboration with Reliance Infocomm.

- Focusing on cargo operations

  Indian Airlines is into the final stages of examining conversion of 5 B737s into freighter aircraft to use them on a hub and spoke concept with Nagpur as a hub to offer express /retail courier services.

  Air India is planning to significantly expand its cargo operations in a phased manner over the next 2 years. For this it plans to dry lease 1 A310 dedicated freighter and one B747 dedicated freighter and convert two A310 aircraft into aircraft for freighter services.

Action Suggested by Research Firm

- *Marketing Strategy*

(a) Although both these players had been improving their services, the general perception in the public eye is still that of inefficient public companies. Therefore, in order to improve the image of IA and AI, an attempt should be made to improve customer care and public relations. More focus on creating customer services station to handle customer queries and other issues. By utilizing IT, customer services can be improved such as making complaints, receiving compensation when appropriate, sending regular updates on services and flights via. SMS text messages.

(b) There should be a sincere attempt to revitalize the promotion mix through aggressive advertising by deploying different media including hoardings/direct mail/internet.

- *HR Strategy*

(a) To prevent poaching problem, IA and AI can enter into no-poaching code with other airlines. Besides this, incentive schemes can be initiated to avoid this problem.

(b) Redeploying the existing staff drawn from non-operational departments like finance and stores to commercial divisions to handle front-line activities.

(c) Enhancing the quality of services by improving on-time performance, the behaviour of front staff, and reservation systems.

- *General Management Strategy*

(a) The civil aviation ministry can also exercise to bring public sector carriers Air India and Indian Airlines together to create a powerhouse that could withstand growing competition. A number of options including merger, putting both airlines under a holding company and simple operational synergy can be considered.

(b) The financial health of Indian Airlines and Air India, though improving, continue to be fragile and they may not be in a position to bear further losses in their market share. For this reason, privatisation of the two airlines could be considered to ensure their continued existence and survival on a commercial basis. This can also affect the working and decision-making of these two players.

- ***Finance Strategy***

  In order to improve the financial conditions of these two players they can go for an IPO to raise funds from general public, this could help to improve the debt-equity ratio and also for funding their expansion plans.

Besides this, these players can also be involved in tie up with other corporate for supporting them to advertise or promote through IA and AI (carrying promotion/ advertisement on glasses, seats, uniform, cabins etc) which can help them to get generate money.

In the light of facts given by Mr. Thulasidas the members wondered that the results of these strategies (if implemented) are for all to see but the officials of two national carriers are still thinking the ways by which they can take AI and IA to new heights. They are making a desperate attempt to restructure and shore up profit. But whether they will be able to resurrect their fortune is a million dollar question.

Questions

1. Identify the key areas that these state-owned players possess that might give them some competitive advantage.(Think about physical assets, social responsibility as well as government support while compiling your list)
2. What strategies would you advise to pursue to deal with the challenges of these two state-owned players in the next five years? (Think about brand building, customer services & CRM etc)
3. Consider the option of combining these two players, will the combined management be stronger or is it likely to become caught up in power struggles and internal and external politics? (Think the advantages in terms of increasing the Indian market presence on the international routes, route rationalization, and better utilization of capacity in domestic and international markets)
4. What is the rationale and strength behind price-reduction adopted by these players? (Think in terms of creating new passenger segments in the domestic and international air travel market).

Annexure

Table 1: Passenger and Cargo Traffic

Year	*No. of Passengers – International and Domestic*	*Freight Traffic*
1970	5.1 million	81,000 tonnes
1998-99	27 million	699,000 tonnes
2001-02	40million	800,000 tonnes
2002-03	43million	979,000 tonnes
2003-04	48million	1,06,8000 tonnes
2004-05	59 million	1,28,9000 tonnes

Source: *media reports*

Table 2: Comparative market share of domestic players

Airline	2004 end	Jan 2006
	Market share in %	
Jet	42	35
Indian + Alliance Ai (subsidiary of IA)	37	25
Sahara	18	11
Air Deccan	1	13
Kingfisher	0	8
Spicejet	0	6
Others	-	2

Source: *Times of India, March 14, 2006.*

Table 3: Future acquisition plan of various players

Airline	*Current fleet size*	*Future acquisitions*
Jet - Sahara	80	Has ordered 10 A330, 10 B777 and 10 B737
Indian + Alliance Air	77	Order for 43 Airbus aircraft to be placed shortly
Air India + Air India Express	44	Has ordered 27 B787, 23 B777 and 18 B737
Kingfisher	9	Has ordered 5 A380, 5 A350, 5 A330, 40 A320 and 35 ATR including options
Air Deccan	24	Has ordered 62 A320 and 30 ATR
Spicejet	5	Has ordered 20 Boeing 737

Table 4 : Foreign Pilots in the Airlines

Name of Airline	*Foreign Pilots*	*Total number of Pilots*	*% of foreign pilots*
Jet Airways	108	780	14
Indian + Alliance Air	19	150	12
Sahara	18	232	8
Air Deccan	140	399	35
Spicejet	9	125	7
Air India	65	615	11
Air India Express	40	80	50
Go Air	23	57	40
Indigo	15	56	27
Paramount Airways	20	35	57

Source: *The Times of India, 4th January 2007.*

EPILOGUE

The stage is set for a merger of Indian Airlines and Air Indian (Times of India, 22.2.2007) in an attempt to arm the two national carries to take on the onslaught from private airlines and large international carries. The new public sector entity will enter the list of top 30 airlines globally and will break into the top 10 in Asia. In his comments on the merger, Mr. Thulasidas said. 'I feel the opportunity offered are huge. First, both airlines would stop competing for passengers by flying on same sectors. With the pooling of resources and integrated network that the merged entity would offer, there would be lot of synergy. We would be able to offer seamless transfers to passengers from any part of India to any part of the globe'. Besides, it could result in redeployment of aircraft since Air India and Indian Airlines are flying on some common routes like Singapore and Dubai.

While the new brand is still to be finalised, Mr. Prafulla Patel, Civil Aviation Minister said the Maharaja could remain the mascot for the merged airlines, while the full-cost domestic and internationals flight would get a similar look in coming years. However, the merger is not going to happen overnight but in a phased manner. There will be one-to-two-year transition period during which many issues will be sorted out. Mr Patel also promised that there would be no lay-offs and the 33,000 employees would remain on the rolls of the new entity.

Table 5 : below gives the fleet facts for the two airlines.

Table 5 : Fleet Facts

	Air India	*Indian Airlines*
Existing Fleet	48	75
Aircraft Ordered	68	43
Employees	15,300	19,300
Revenues (Rs cr)	9,677	6,000
Profit (Rs cr)	16.50	49.00
Pilots	615	700
Passengers (millions)	4.4	8.0
Market Share (%)	20	20*
Number of destinations		
Domestic	13	54
International	48	18

* Indian Airlines has a 12% share of the international traffic.

- **Source:** *Times of India, 22.2.2007*

CASE 4

JAGRUT GRAHAK MANDAL, PATAN

Dr J Pancholi, Middlesex University, London, UK.
Dr A Modi, S K School of Business Management,
Hemachandracharya North Gujarat University, Patan, Gujarat. INDIA.

Abstract

This case study emphasizes on management accounting system of a non-government organization (NGO) which is operating into voluntary service sector in western part of India. Jagrut Grahak Mandal (JGM) is an organization established to create awareness of the consumers, investors and general public and there by serve the society. This case attempts to analyze the management accounting practices of an NGO and tries to highlight the intricacies of an NGO's responsibility towards it stakeholders such as donors, members, regulator authorities, and the society at large. The case highlights different perspectives of accounting and introduces contemporary model of the Balanced Score Card.

Introduction and Background

Jagrut Grahak Mandal (JGM) located in Patan district in the North Gujarat region of western India is registered as a Public Trust since 14th October, 1985. (Appendix-I and II). It is permanently recognized by Food and Civil Supply Department Gujarat state since 19th March, 1991 and grantable continuously since 1987. It is one of the only nine such 'Investors' Association' all over India which are granted by Securities and Exchange Board of India (SEBI). SEBI is the supreme most authority of government of India to control and regulate capital markets.

JGM started with 10 members committee in 1985, then onwards Mr. T. D. Mehta has been elected as a president. Today in 2006, he is of 80 years old and yet he is very hard working and energetic social activist. He cannot tolerate corruption and malpractices done by the traders and companies and as a result many of the cases are still pending in the consumer court of India.

Acknowledgements:

Our special thanks to Mr T D Mehta (Founder, Jagrut Grahak Mandal, Patan, India) and Dr B A Prajapati (Director, S K School of Business Management, Hemachandracharya North Gujarat University, Patan, India) for their continuous guidance and intellectual inputs.

JGM has been successful in receiving the grants from SEBI because of Ms. Krisna Virani, who had endeavoured in taking the approval from SEBI. Ms. Krisna Virani (Master of Social Welfare) is a new employee of JGM since 2001.

JGM is representing in the district Advisory committee of civil supply and Consumer affairs since last 14 years. JGM has conducted large number of seminars on Consumer' awareness focusing on food adulteration, unfair practices of local retail traders, unethical behaviour of dealers and big corporations by publishing many legal books and monthly magazines. As soon as it has been approved by SEBI under - one among the nine Investor Associations all over India, it has imparted many programmes to create awareness to the public in vernacular language of Gujarati and also popular languages of Hindi and English. From the year 2001-02 onwards it has organized many workshops, seminars on Investor awareness by providing guidance to the general public of many towns and villages in Gujarat. It has also published on its own, journals, magazines and monthly reviews for social, consumer and investor awareness.

Even when events do not end up in consumer court there are substantial reputation risks to JGM and donors will reduce their funding to JGM in then even of loss of reputation. It is observed from last five years that one winning case adds 2% more sponsorship of funds from the next year onwards and one failure case may reduce the funding by 5% from the next year onwards.

JGM is also very active in networking with other organizations and has conducted many seminars and programmes jointly with Banks, Association of Stock Brokers, Colleges, Dairies, Alumni Associations, etc. In the year 2001-02 JGM organised a seminar on challenges of stock market in India's largest Dairy - Mother Dairy, Mehsana with SKSBM Alumni Association, an active alumni association of a local business school in a university at Patan.

1. Financial Management and Accounting System

With an increasing emphasis from donors on transparency and regulating mechanism affecting non government organizations (NGOs), JGM is realizing the importance of having a sound finance and accounting function supporting all organizational activities. Building this stable accounting and finance function, a Finance Personnel Mr. Joseph working at JGM has tried to acquire adequate knowledge and capabilities in the field of finance and accounting. The Financial and Management system for JGM aims at to manage the financial activities in such a way that all the financial resources can be optimally utilized for social, environmental or human welfare and awareness purposes. Obviously, profit maximization is not a motive. However, the resource optimization is always an objective for JGM. The financial management in JGM is aimed to develop and share tools and techniques to improve budgeting, financial analysis, management controls, cost effectiveness and the sustainability of nonprofits.

An expert in financial and accounting system of a NGO, Ms Shami Sheth was invited from the UK with reference to a common friend of Mr T D Mehta. She was overwhelmed with the activities of JGM in her visit to Patan. In her report, she narrated how she felt that many multinational NGOs yet need to learn a lot from JGM which is based in a small town named Patan in India. She also mentioned - "The objective of financial management and accounting system of a NGO is to create a more meaningful relationship between the donors, members, board, beneficiaries, the government and other stake holders...."

2. Financial Accounting: Reporting and System at JGM

The following are the main financial accounting and management reports generated through out the year, as and when demanded by the President .

- Donor Level consolidated receipts.
- Project wise utilization of funds.
- Project wise comparative expenses report for three consecutive years.
- Project wise Balance Sheet, Income and Expenses, Receipts and Payments and Day Books.
- Account wise Receipts and Payments, Date wise, Weekly, Monthly, Quarterly, Half and Full yearly.

Further, if any donor-wise report is required by the President then it is generated by the accountant Mr. Pandey.

3. Future Planning

A common view is that the JGM has entirely separate planning requirements from the commercial operation and that the analytical framework developed for one has no applications in the other. JGM can relate each segment of their operation to the relevant benchmark, and incorporate action planning on a year by year basis as is best practice with the commercial plan.

JGM plays a major role in the development of the community in Patan and many other villages and small town in and around Patan. The Government provides financial assistance for organising workshops/seminars which helps to disseminate research findings, identify problems areas, discuss problems and identify research needs. etc, in the broad field of social welfare, social policy and social development. Government grants from SEBI and the Department of Company Affairs are released after 3 months on approval and after getting the project budget from concerned NGOs.

Mr. Mehta understands and believes that the cash-flow is always uncertain and sensitively generated on the sets of assumptions. However, considerable variations are possible. Below, Mr. Joseph identifies a number of factors that could impact cash flow, the factors which may effect are like - Grant may not be received from the year

2003 onwards. Grant may be received fully or half of applied in time. Accountant is of the opinion that many times it happens that grant may be received after a year.

4. The Dilemma

Ms. Shami Sheth in her study of various NGOs in western part of India found that there was an increasingly urgent need for NGOs to professionalize their management practices. The fact that the organizations are not with a motive to make profits, does not exempt them to practise professional management. She presented similar views in the report submitted to JGM. In her study of around 3 months at JGM, she also presented her findings (Table 1) of preliminary of ranking of the most acute problems of NGOs in western India. This study also highlighted possibility of application of latest measurement tool named 'The Balanced Score Card', propounded by Prof. Robert Kaplan and Mr. David Norton, USA.

Table 1: A study of preliminary ranking of most acute problems in NGOs

Problem description	Probability for the problem to be chosen = absolute weight of the problem (multiple choice)
Poor relations with central governing bodies and authorities	0.80
Limited access to legal information	0.49
Lack of consumer supports	0.45
Lack or absence of reliable environmental and social information	0.40
Poor accounting skills	0.30
Lack of special environmental training	0.20
Lack of volunteer support	0.51
General legal problems	0.27
Poor financial support	0.70
Lack of business skills	0.19
Poor financial skills	0.58
Poor relations with local authorities	0.18
Poor horizontal networking with other NGOs	0.55
Weak administration of JGM	0.12
Poor public relations	0.55
Other problems	0.08

Vouchers (Appendix III and IV) are the documents made by an enterprise which gives evidence of a financial Transaction. Similar process is at JGM. These vouchers are to be accompanied by supporting external documents like, memos, applications, receipts etc. Number of financial transaction per year is very limited at JGM, approximately 130, having a huge quantity of funds utilisation. President has appointed a management accountant Mr. Joshi from the Financial year 2001-02 onwards for their book keeping and accounts finalization.

Mr. T D Mehta entrusted responsibilities of studying financial accounting system at JGM to all three of the staff - Mr. Pandey, Mr. Joseph and Mr. Joshi. Mr. Pandey, accountant of JGM, has prepared the Balance sheet, Income and Expenditure account in the following manner by treating Grants as liabilities:

Table 2: Balance Sheet as at 31st March 2002

Liabilities	**Rs. (Lakhs*)**	**Assets**	**Rs. (Lakhs*)**
Corpus	0.10		
Surplus	0.30		
State Govt. Grant	17.20	Building	1.00
Consumer Surksha Grant	1.00	Cash and Bank	28.50
Creditors	2.90		
Grant from SEBI and Others			
Opening Balance 5.00			
Add: Recd. this year 20.00			
Less: Spent this year 17.00			
Closing Balance	8.00		
Total	**29.50**	**Total**	**29.50**

*1 Lakh = 100,000

Table 3: Income and Expenditure Account for year ended 31st March 2002

Expenses	**Rs. (Lakhs*)**	**Income**	**Rs. (Lakhs*)**
Printing and Stationary charges	0.10	Life membership fees	0.15
Monthly Publication	0.30	Life subscription fees	0.10
Office rent	0.10		
Salaries	0.60	Donations	1.05
Other expenses	0.05	Misc. Income (Interest)	0.15
Surplus	0.30		
Total	1.45	Total	1.45

* 1 Lakh = 100,000

Tablet 4: Receipts and Payments Account for year ended 31st March 2002

Receipts	Rs. (Lakhs*)	Payments	Rs. (Lakhs*)
Opening Balance	7.00	Program Expenses #	17.00
Grant from SEBI and Others	20.00	Office rent	0.10
Life membership fees**	0.15	Monthly Publication	0.30
Life subscription fees***	0.10	Printing and Stationery charges	0.10
State Govt. Grant	17.20	Salaries	0.60
Consumer Surksha Grant	1.00	Other expenses	0.05
Donations	1.05	Closing Balance	28.50
Misc. Income (Interest)	0.15		
Total	**46.65**	**Total**	**46.65**

* 1 Lakh = 100,000

** JGM on taking life membership fees fights the case in to court on behalf of the members.

***JGM issues monthly review to the subscription members.

\# Program Expenses includes seminar expenses, awareness expenses and other social development expenses.

However, disagreeing to what Mr. Pandey has prepared, Mr. Joseph, Finance Officer, feels that the grants are to be treated as Income. Mr. Joseph has prepared the statements in the following manner.

Table 5: Balance Sheet as at 31st March 2002

Liabilities	Rs.(Lakhs*)	Assets	Rs. (Lakhs*)
Corpus	0.10	Building	1.00
Creditors	2.90	Cash and Bank	28.50
Surplus			
Opening Balance 5.00			
Add. For the year 21.50			
Closing Balance	26.50		
Total	**29.50**	**Total**	**29.50**

Table 6: Income and Expenditure Account for year ended 31st March 2002

Expenses	Rs. (Lakhs*)	Income	Rs. (Lakhs*)
Program Expenses	17.00	Grant from SEBI and Others	20.00
Printing and Stationery charges	0.10	Life membership fees**	0.15
Monthly Publication	0.30	Life subscription fees***	0.10
Office rent	0.10	State Govt. Grant	17.20
Salaries	0.60	Consumer Surksha Grant	1.00
Other expenses	0.05	Donations	1.05
Surplus	21.50	Misc. Income (Interest)	0.15
Total	**39.65**	**Total**	**39.65**

* 1 Lakh = 100,000

Mr. Joseph, finance officer believes that the Receipts and Payments Account is not affected, and hence he agrees with that prepared by Mr. Pandey.

However, Mr. Joshi, management accountant believes that that grant should be considered as 'conditional income'. Mr. Joshi prepared the final accounts as given below:

Table 7: Balance Sheet as at 31st March 2002

Liabilities	Rs. (Lakhs *)	Assests	Rs. (Lakhs *)
Corpus	0.10	Building	1.00
Surplus	0.30		
Creditors	2.90		
Unspent Grants :			
SEBI and Others	8.00		
State Govt. Grant	17.20	Cash and Bank	28.50
Consumer Surksha Grant	1.00		
Total	**29.50**	**Total**	**29.50**

* 1 Lakh = 100,000

Table 8: Income and Expenditure Account for year ended 31st March 2002

Expenses	Rs. (Lakhs *)	Income	Rs. (Lakhs *)
Program Expenses	17.00	*Grant from SEBI and Others*	
Office Rent	0.10	Received this year *20.00*	
Salaries	0.60	*Add:* unspent balance brought forward from previous year *5.00*	
Other expenses	0.05	*Less* : Unspent balance at end of year carried forward *8.00*	
Printing and Stationery	0.10	Balance grant for the year	17.00
Monthly Publication	0.30	Life membership fees*	0.15
Surplus	0.30	Life subscription fees**	0.10
		Donations	1.05
		Misc. Income (Interest)	0.15
Total	**18.45**	**Total**	**18.45**

* 1 Lakh = 100,000

Further, the accounts were also prepared by Mr. Joseph for the year ending 31st March, 2003.

Table 9: Balance sheet as at 31st March 2003

Liabilities	Rs. (Lakhs*)	Assets	Rs. (Lakhs*)
Corpus	0.10	Building	1.00
Creditors	2.90		
I and E Account		Cash and Bank	10.50
Opening Balance 26.50			
Less: Deficit for the year 18.00			
Closing Balance	8.50		
Total	**11.50**	**Total**	**11.50**

* 1 Lakh = 100,000

Table 10: Income and Expenditure Account for year ended 31st March 2003

Expenses	Rs. (Lakhs*)	Income	Rs. (Lakhs*)
Program Expenses	17.50	Grant from SEBI and Others	14.00
Printing and Stationery	0.10	Life membership fees	0.15
Monthly Publication	0.30	Life subscription fees	0.10
Office Rent	0.10	Donations	1.00
Salaries	0.60	Misc. Income (Interest)	0.75
Other expenses	0.40	Deficit	18.00
State Govt. Grant Exp.	14.00		
Consumer Surksha Grant	1.00		
Total	**34.00**	**Total**	**34.00**

* 1 Lakh = 100,000

Table 11: Receipts and Payments Account for year ended 31st March 2003

Receipts	Rs. (Lakhs*)	Payments	Rs. (Lakhs*)
Opening Balance	28.50	Program Expenses	17.50
Grant from SEBI and Others	14.00	Program Exp. State Gov. Grant	14.00
Life membership fees**	0.15	Printing and Stationery	0.10
Life subscription fees***	0.10	Monthly Publication	0.30
Donations	1.00	Office Rent	0.10
Misc. Income (Interest)	0.75	Salaries	0.60
		Other expenses	0.40
		Consumer Surksha Grant Exp.	1.00
		Closing Balance	10.50
Total	**44.5**	**Total**	**44.5**

* 1 Lakh = 100,000

Mr. Mehta, president of JGM is confused for finalisation of their books of accounts for the year ended 2003. He also surprised that nobody has given tax treatment on the finalization of Income Statement. Tax-exempted organizations in India have to spend at least 85% of their annual income each year as per the law. Mr. Mehta is also in a dilemma that which method is to be followed, that can present the fair results of a NGO. Mr. Mehta is curious to know the actual position of JGM. Mr. Mehta says that Grants are decreasing year by year at 30%. It is also said that by political change in the Gujarat State, the future state grants may not be available

Appendix: I

Registered as Public Trust Since 1985 : Registration No.: F/763/Patan

Spl. C/C/BPT 2.

№ 10769

નોંધણીનો દાખલો

આથી દાખલો આપવામાં આવે છે કે હેઠળ જણાવેલા સાર્વજનિક ટ્રસ્ટને સને ૧૯૫૦ ના મુંબઈના સાર્વજનિક ટ્રસ્ટો બાબતના (સન ૧૯૫૦ ના મુંબઈના ૨૯ માં) અધિનિયમ અન્વયે મહેસાણા ખાતેની સાર્વજનિક ટ્રસ્ટ નોંધણી કચેરીમાં યોગ્ય રીતે નોંધવામાં આવ્યું છે.

સાર્વજનિક ટ્રસ્ટનું નામ જાગૃત ગ્રાહક મંડળ, પાટણ

સાર્વજનિક ટ્રસ્ટોના રજિસ્ટરમાંના નંબર એફ/૭૬૩/પાટણ

કોને દાખલો આપ્યો તે ત્રિલોકભાઈ બી. મહેતા

સરદાર પટેલ કોલેજ સામે, ગુંગડીવાડી, પાટણ

મારી સહીથી આજ તારીખ માહે સને ૧૯૯...... ને દિને આપ્યો 18 MAR 2002

જુનો નોંધણી નંબર: એફ/૩૧૭/મહે

નોંધણી તારીખ: ૧૭/૧૦/૮૫

સહી M. L. Kalaria

હોદ્દો મદદનીશ ચેરિટી કમિશનર

મહેસાણા પ્રદેશ, મહેસાણા.

Appendix: II

Registered as Society Since 1985 : Registration No. Guj/463/Patan

Spl./R. s./1 g.

No. 3663

નોંધણીનો દાખલો

સને ૧૮૬૦નો મંડળીઓની નોંધણી બાબતનો અધિનિયમ

(સને ૧૮૬૦નો ૨૧મો અધિનિયમ)

નોંધણી નંબર ગુજ/૪૬૩/પાટણ

આથી દાખલો આપવામાં આવે છે કે જાગૃત ગ્રાહક મંડળ ને

પાટણ

આજ .... તારીખે, મંડળીઓની નોંધણી બાબતના (સન ૧૮૬૦ ના ૨૧માં)

અધિનિયમ અન્વયે, યોગ્ય રીતે નોંધવામાં આવી છે.

મારી સહીથી આજ 18 MAR 2002 સન ૨૦૦ ને દિને આપ્યો.

જુની નોંધણી નંબર: ગુજ ૩૨૧ મહે

નોંધણી તારીખ: ૧૪/૧૦/૮૫

N.L. Kalera

મંડળીઓની નોંધણીના આસિસ્ટન્ટ રજિસ્ટ્રાર,

.... વિભાગ

મહેસાણા

Appendix: III

VOUCHER OF JAGRUT GRAHAK MANDAL

Nr. Subhas Chok, PATAN, GUJARAT.
JOURNAL VOUCHER

DATE : ____________ Voucher Number : __________________

ACCOUNT HEAD

DEBIT (Rs) CREDIT (R

TOTAL

Narration ---

Appendix: IV

JAGRUT GRAHAK MANDAL,
Nr. Subhas Chok, PATAN, GUJARAT
CASH PAYMENT VOUCHER

DATE : ___________ Voucher Number : _________
Payee : _________________________________

____

ACCOUNT HEAD

DEBIT (Rs)

TOTAL (Rs)

Narration --

________ ____________ ____________ ________
____
Payer Accountant Approved By Folio Number Payee Sign.
Revenue Stamp

Questions:

1. Who are different stakeholders in a NGO? How their expectations from accounting information is diverse? Why?
2. How raising of finance in a NGO is different then a corporate organization? How JGM is raising its finance? Explain what are the reporting implications of this difference.
3. Critically evaluate various methods suggested by Mr. Pandey, Mr. Joseph and Mr. Joshi? Which method would you like to choose if you are head of this organization? Why?
4. Critically explain the issues emerging related to control and reporting system in a NGO.
5. Explain the meaning of Balanced Scorecard. How is it applicable to a NGO particularly to JGM?
6. What would you do if you are Mr. T D Mehta? Why?

CASE 5

SUCCESSION PLANNING IN FAMILY BUSINESS
THE GENDER ANGLE:
THE CASE OF MEHTA STEEL

Dr B M Kacholia
NMIMS University, Mumbai, India.

Abstract

This case deals with a human dilemma and a relatively unexplored but important aspect of succession. With business-owning families getting smaller in size, with daughters getting good education, business aspirations of female children are also rising, especially in families with no male off springs. The issue of succession in such families is highlighted in this case.

Introduction

Mehta Steel Pvt. Ltd. is a great story of sheer hard work, guts and enterprise of one man, Rakesh Mehta, who left his village in Uttar Pradesh and came to the then Bombay, in 1971, in search of a livelihood. His family's financial position was quite weak and he had to give up hopes of further education after finishing his high school. In Bombay, he took up whatever small/temporary jobs came his way and also found a 'shelter' in a far-off suburb of Bombay. He had to not only support himself but also save some money for his family members in Uttar Pradesh. But he was determined to keep struggling and trying to find a stable job. He had not only heard of but also seen how Bombay could change one's fortunes. He saw the immense possibilities of realizing his dreams by working hard - with a lot of perseverance and some luck thrown in.

The first stroke of good luck in his uneventful life was the landing of a job in a firm trading in Iron and Steel in the Masjid Bunder area. He had to work as a helper-cum-clerk.

But Rakesh did not mind. For the first time, he was getting to know a particular business and gradually, understand its intricacies. He worked hard and soon came to know all the important traders and consumers of steel market and had become a familiar face in the market.

In 1975, he took the first major step on an independent career path, by leaving his job. Making use of his close knowledge of the market and acquaintance with market men, he started working as a broker in the steel market - a profession where you need to have a lot of goodwill and liasoning skills but no capital investment.

This was only the first major career move and the second one was soon to follow. In 1977, just 6 years after landing in Bombay, he again upped himself and set up his own firm trading in Iron & Steel, in the name and style of "Mehta Steel Corporation". And from there on, it was a steady upward climb. In 1986, he moved into his own office from a rented cabin space.

Rakesh was quite happy expanding his trading business and enjoying life with his family - his wife and their three daughters. Meanwhile another trading firm 'Mehta Traders' was also established in 1989.

In the year 1995, he made another major move towards firmly establishing himself as an entrepreneur by getting into manufacturing. From businessman/trader to an industrialist - a move involving not only higher risks but also calling upon a different set of entrepreneurial skills and qualities. But the young lad from Uttar Pradesh had by now gathered enough knowledge, confidence and experience to try his hand on a much bigger canvas.

He purchased 7.5 acres of land near Pune and set up 'Mehta Steel Pvt. Ltd.' with a plant capacity to manufacture 10,000 tons of steel products per annum. Manufacturing commenced in 1996. The range of products was initially confined only to the more popular ones. Rakesh's intimate knowledge of the steel market was a great asset and he successfully catered to the rising demand - gradually adding capacity and widening the range of products. He branded his product as "SONA" and gradually established it well in the domestic market. Meanwhile he got the ISI Mark for its quality standards. Sales grew from Rs. 3.5 crores in the year 1996-97 to Rs. 30 crores in 2004-05, an extremely creditable achievement in a heavy engineering sector, where raw material prices and availability, both fluctuated widely.

The spectacular success of Mehta Steel, spurred on Rakesh to drive himself harder and wish for more. He had always worked ceaselessly and every upward step was a testimony to his business acumen. It only gave him one more opportunity to prove himself. He presided over his own 'creations' with single-minded devotion and also total control.

In the year 2003-2004, he acquired additional manufacturing facilities by taking over a steel manufacturing plant with a total production capacity of 10,000 tons per annum.

Organization Structure

Like all owner-driven organizations, Mehta Group is also an owner-centric organization, with a great deal of centralized decision-making. And it seems to have been quite 'effective' in terms of capacity as well as turnover growth. Success has also created a strong belief in the mind of this hardy entrepreneur that his style of organizing and managing his business, is the most suitable for achieving his goals. (Afterall, nothing succeeds like success). He gives the necessary freedom to his men who achieve the targets set by him. He works on a 'cost plus' method.

He has built a need-based, lean structure. He is the CMD of his company with his wife and one family friend as Directors.

The working set-up below looks something like this –

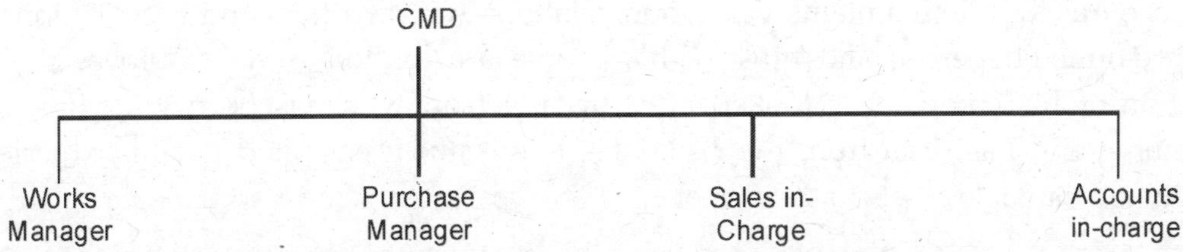

The Family in Management

Besides, Rakesh, his second daughter Madhu, is the only one of his three daughters - who is actively interested in pursuing a career in her family business and is gradually getting herself more involved with it. The eldest daughter is married, resides abroad and she or her husband are not interested in the management of her father's business. The youngest one is still a student. Mrs. Mehta is not actively involved in the management of the family business.

Besides the above members of his own family, Rakesh recruited one of his nephews (his elder brother's son) in 1998 to look after purchases and also liaise with the sales in-charge. Rakesh's need for a trusted and 'own' person to share his growing responsibility is quite understandable since there is no male child of his own. His young nephew has picked up his work well and has proved himself worthy of Rakesh's trust. He is paid a fixed salary plus commission on procurement of material on per ton basis. This is more to help him build his own assets. However, he is neither professionally qualified, nor very high on other qualities of a modern manager.

With the acquisition of the new steel plant, Rakesh may persuade his other two nephews also to join his business. The logic again is to have his own family members around to share growing responsibilities. However, the two nephews are pursuing their own careers and have not expressed any interest in joining their uncle. Rakesh being the most successful member of the family feels a great sense of attachment and responsibility towards other family members and wishes to ensure a good future for them.

The Present Management Scenario

Rakesh's intimate knowledge of the steel market has always guided him to work hard for complete customer satisfaction. His product is of top quality and his dream is to make Mehta Steel as reputed a name as Tata Steel. He has consistently produced ISI quality products and is now working towards achieving an ISO certification. His plant has achieved zero rejection quality standards and there are no customer complaints about quality. Orders are executed promptly and delivery schedules are strictly maintained.

He has empowered his managers to a reasonable extent but he remains the central power figure. We can call his management style 'paternalistic'. Suggestions from all levels are encouraged. He maintains very good relations with workers and their Union. He is a welfare-oriented person and most of his people are his long-time employees. The sales function of his company is looked after by a person who has been with him since the beginning and has risen from the ranks. He is not much educated but his experience and loyalty are valuable assets to the owner.

He employs local people in his factory, unlike some other factories in the area which have hired a large number of migrant workers and have faced labour trouble.

The Industry

The Steel industry has many major players. Mehta Steel's market share is growing. Their products are sold well and have multiple uses in heavy industry, construction, fabrication, etc.

Exports vs. Domestic Demand

Mehta Steel's total current production is absorbed in the local market and hence they are not keen to take on the botheration of exporting. However, they have recently become a member of the Engineering Export Promotion Council (EEPC).

Actual Working

The company's turnover has grown steadily and their 2004-2005 sales touched Rs.30 crores.

It did experience working capital and debt-servicing difficulties in the past but the situation is now much improved. The company has excellent relations with the bankers as it has always honoured its commitments.

With growing business, it is experiencing a shortage of office space. It would like to not only have a bigger place but a more modern office set-up as well. The younger generation is quite keen on modernizing the office set-up, and Mehta may reluctantly agree, although he does not see any 'need' for it.

Personnel (Staff) Training

There are no formal personnel policies and required staff is hired on the basis of recommendations and experience. As mentioned, most of the staff members are working in the company for the last many years. Training is actually "working on the job" and interacting with the owner. There is no other formal training. Loyalty takes precedence over 'professional' qualifications. This approach has worked very well so far and Rakesh has no complaints on this front.

Among the owner's family members, only his second daughter Madhu has done a post-graduate management course and is preparing herself for greater organizational responsibilities. She feels that in spite of their success so far, there is a lack of professionalism in management and staff needs to be better qualified and trained.

However, Rakesh does not feel any need for changing his management style since he is 'doing quite well'. People who have been working with him for years - both in Production function and Sales function, are those who have grown with him and are strong on experience and loyalty. Procurement is looked after by his nephew.

The Succession Issue

Mehta Steel has had a great run of success and Rakesh's has been a classic tale of an entrepreneur building from scratch. He is still a youthful 54, and the issue of nominating and preparing a successor to take over the reins at some future date, seem to be still quite distant.

But this is not unusual. Every entrepreneur who has built the business with his own blood and sweat, does not allow the 'distant' issues like succession to divert his attention from the 'immediate' entrepreneurial tasks - such as expansions, diversification, achieving higher targets of sales, profits and 'personal glory' through greater achievements. After all, it is not a 'pleasant' thought to think of your own 'retirement' or mortality. There is a hidden desire to carry on till the end. And the feeling that, there is 'ample time' still to think about these things later is quite common among entrepreneurs. (We shall cross the bridge when we come to it).

But perpetuation of a family business is different from an individual traveller coming to and crossing a bridge. It needs a great amount of advance planning and preparation. Then only can the entrepreneur hope to perpetuate the work of his life-time and achieve "immortality". Lack of succession planning and preparation has landed many an organization in serious troubles. This has happened to large family businesses abroad as well to those nearer home.

"It is difficult to accept that our life is finite and that the world will continue without us. Despite our narcissism, we are still one of many and the universe does not recognize our specialness; we are subject to the same laws of nature as everyone else".[1]

In the words of Leon Denco, one of the world's foremost family business consultants "(succession) disaster occurs because the owner of the business cannot face the fact that at some point he must and will be replaced. If the successful business owner, who had the ability, vision and guts to build the business from nothing, does not have the courage to face the problems of the future, then his banker and attorney will do it ".[2]

Research abroad has shown that firms with well-planned succession tend to be more profitable after succession than those with no succession plan in place.

It is, therefore, obvious that a forward-looking entrepreneur not only does not think of himself as irreplaceable, but plans for a successor well in time so that he/she could imbibe the organization culture and the softer skills of running the family business, besides learning the ropes of it.

The Succession Issue at Mehta Steel : The Gender Angle

As already mentioned, Mr. Mehta has three daughters and his second daughter, Madhu, is quite keen on joining her father's business and, eventually to take over its entire management. (A male sibling would have been the 'automatic' heir apparent).

Now, the thought of having a female child successor, howsoever, qualified and interested - she may be in handling the family business, still does not get an easy approval in the Indian business family circles. Although times are changing, many family business owners around the world and more so, in oriental societies, still see the choice of a daughter as successor, as something to be avoided. The reasons are usual - marriage, son-in-law entering the business, possible change in the established name and title of business, the fear of nephews being side-lined in future, the extent of her own role in business post-marriage, and so on.

However, there are strong signals emanating from some cases of married daughters doing extremely well as successors. They have strong academic credentials as well as leadership talent and great inter-personal skills. Besides, the number of female owner-managers is also on the rise. These trends are now quite visible on Indian business scenario, too.

"No longer should women be ignored as contenders for the top slots in family firms because of their gender. Successors to the throne should be considered based on the right combination of characteristics".[3] However, it is a fact that many family business founders simply find it too difficult to decide on and 'declare' a daughter as the successor, and prefer to live on with ambiguity, rather than take the bull by the horns. "It is unfortunate that gender stereotypes still exist but they remain a fact of life – stereotypes can create an unfair disadvantage for woman".[3]

In many cases, this state of ambiguity may be prolonged because the father, while genuinely believing in the capabilities of his daughter, may not really want her to face the multiple headaches of employee problems, suppliers and customers related tricky issues, travelling on business, fluctuating economic environment affecting the fortunes of family business, labour unions, etc. As a loving parent, the father may not want to think of her being troubled by all these 'bothersome' issues. "The idea of appointing women as heirs - apparent still disturbs a significant number of older male owners……..some owners may even prefer to bring aboard sons-in-law, sell their business or have nonfamily males succeed them rather than pass the business on to a daughter……. It's not a matter of thinking their daughters are less qualified to run the business; rather they may not want their daughters to be bothered with business-related headaches. Sexist or not, it's reality in many cases".

Rakesh would also rather have her enjoy the fruits of his hard work - the wealth he has created and the good life which he can ensure for her as a married and well-settled child rather than opt for the hard work and headaches of running a heavy industry. The choice of a successor to manage a heavy industry may still fall on a male relative or the son-in-law and in extreme cases where there is no male heir or he is not interested in the family business, sell-off may be the only option.

It is also possible that as a father he may have doubts about a girl succeeding in a heavy industry, seen as a male domain. Parental thinking seems to be more positive where the family business relates to 'softer' businesses like financial or I.T. services. In some cases, a father may even discourage his daughter from entering his heavy industry business and encourage and help her to start her own independent business in a 'softer' area.

A twist in the tale

Madhu not only sees herself as a 'natural successor' but is equipping herself for the job by getting post-graduate management education as well as by taking keen interest in her father's business. Her father appreciates her work and is very proud of his daughter. In our personal discussions with him on this subject, he was quite open to the idea of his daughter being his successor. (However, the future issues like post-marriage career goals of the daughter, still remain in undiscussed). He is open to giving his daughter enough scope to try her new ideas after her management education. He seems to be open to ideas from all sources. He shows great tolerance for mistakes. However, there is no visible plan to groom her as his successor.

Besides, the succession issue in this particular case has one more dimension, which makes it a classic 'Catch-22' situation.

As mentioned earlier, his nephew (his brother's son), has been associated with his business as a Manager in-charge of Purchases for the last five years. He has been taking keen interest in his work and Rakesh and the family are satisfied with his performance. He is a familiar figure at Mehta Steel and all its business associates (customers, suppliers) as well as employees; know that he is a member of the owner's family. They also know that Rakesh has no male issue, that his one daughter is already married and settled abroad. The second daughter, Madhu, is seen as a young girl who is taking interest in the business as long as she is not married but will eventually get married and discontinue working in the family business. She is not 'perceived' as the future successor to Rakesh heading the family business, although some business associates are appreciative of her calibre and personal qualities.

It must be said to his credit that the nephew has never tried to promote the impression that he is a possible successor. Rakesh has emphasized during our discussions that the nephew will have to go up in his career solely on merit and his nephew or nephews do not expect or aspire to becoming owners or even part-owners in future.

So, the issue is not so much of ownership as of actually heading and managing the business by the owner's daughter. Prolonged uncertainty about succession may dent Madhu's self-confidence, and she is already feeling confused about her future role.

Some solution will have to found to resolve the issue so that (i) the eligible and qualified daughter gets an opportunity to prove herself; (ii) Rakesh is reasonably assured that his business will be managed very well by his successor; (iii) that the family is assured of keeping the family ownership and wealth; and (iv) the nephew gets due recognition and reward for his hard work (in the absence of which he may not extend fullest co-operation to the successor or may leave the organization).

Foot Notes:

1 *"The Myth of Tomorrow" by Gary Buffone, - Tata McGraw-Hill 2003 Edition.*

2 *Quoted by Manfred Kets De Vries in his "Family Business - Human Dilemmas in the Family Firm"*

3 *The Family Business Answer Book' Barbara B. Buchholz, Margaret Crane & Ross W. Nager (Prentice - Hall Press) 1999.*

Questions:

If you are called in as a management consultant.

1. What would be your advice to Rakesh to tackle the succession issue and come out with a solution which will be good for the family and good for the family business? Please remember, as of today he professes open-mindedness on the issue of his daughter succeeding him.
2. What follow-up steps will have to be taken to ensure that the suggested solution is put into practice effectively - (i) steps to be taken immediately in Rakesh's life time as the head of business and (ii) a plan of action for the period following that.
3. Besides the above issues, why has Rakesh so far not leveraged his well-established goodwill and product brand to achieve greater professionalization and diversification? Would you consider it a case of "satisfactory underperformance"? Or is Rakesh afraid of losing total control, if he professionalises his business?
4. Could you suggest some steps for future, taking into consideration all the facts of the case, could you suggest some concrete steps for the future stability and growth of Mehta Steel - a sort of Business Plan (Short term as well as medium term)?

EPILOGUE

The present case study is of a family business where the founder does not have a male heir. However, when one or more male siblings are there, a family business founder may think that "our daughter would do the best job, but we have to offer the business to our first-born son".[1]

We made a small study, involving some of our female students of family business - a few with one or/more male siblings and a few with no male sibling. Numerically, it was not a very large sample but the interaction with both these groups of female students did give us some leads for further research.

From this study it appears that they all are very eager to play a larger role in their family businesses and are very confident of meeting all the challenges. They want to use their talent in expanding and diversifying their family business. Even after marriage they would like to be involved with their in-laws businesses (many hope to marry in business families) although they may or may not make it a full-time career.

Those who do not have a male sibling are quite sure of succeeding their father & do not think that being a girl will any way be a hindrance to their success. They would like to ensure this by making it clear to their future in-laws / husbands. Some said they will even sacrifice marriage, if need be.

They are all confident that their management education will enable them to develop a team of professionals to work with them in running the business well. Some think it may be possible that their husbands may join them in running their father's business or a male cousin may join. However, others do not want their husbands / in-laws to come in. They want to run the show as its head, with the support of professional managers.

It should be kept in mind that all the female students were in their early twenties and their fathers are still in late 40s or early 50s. The issue of succession still seems to be a long way off. The eventual succession event may or may not be in keeping with the current thinking of the families or the daughters. situations and goals may change with the passage of time.

However, as of now women's dreams are more vulnerable than men's in all male-dominated cultures. What business families can do is to support their daughters by

I. giving them good education and instilling confidence in them.

II. allowing them to take risks appropriate to their achievements.

III. helping them in defining realistic goals and supporting them to achieve those.

IV. offering them continuous reinforcement for their achievements.

"Family-owned businesses need to give an equal chance to their daughters to enter the Family Business. If everyone makes a genuine effort, a day will come when we will not just have "Mukherjee & sons" and "Pestonjee & sons" but also "Mukherjee & Daughters" and "Pestonjee & Daughters".[2]

One thing is now obvious. We are likely to see the emergence of more and more women as heads of their family businesses. They are equipping themselves with technical and management qualifications and together with their natural feminine qualities, they hope to lead their family businesses to greater successes. In a number of business families, even in the 'traditional' Indian Society, they have acquitted themselves well and have proved their capabilities.

"In the charmed world of popular television serials, women are still largely confined to their homes in business families, but perhaps it will not be long before the serials catch up with reality. An erosion of old joint family values, a penchant for higher education and a general surge in confidence among women are giving rise to more daughters and daughters-in-law of traditional families taking up higher-profile corporate roles. The men are not complaining". (Hindustan Times, 23.9.2006)

"Today, there are several reasons why daughters and daughters-in-law are assuming leadership positions in traditional family companies which could include the lack of male heir, higher education in specialised subjects, or having an aptitude for management".[3]

The Hindustan Times report also quotes Dr. Gita Piramal, Corporate Historian "The issue of succession had gained prominence with the emergence of more and more nuclear families among traditional business houses......... family patriarchs looked for capable leaders and did not worry about the gender".[4]

(In the absence of a male heir, Mr. K.K. Birla's three married daughters will inherit the control of his group companies. Same in case of Dr. Reddy of Apollo Hospitals and the Jumbo Group of Dubai, owned by late Mr. Manu Chhabria).

However, it may be a bit too early to think that there is already gender parity in traditional societies, although a change is visible in many large business houses and also some medium and small family enterprises. They are giving their daughters an equal opportunities to acquire the best of education in technical as well as management fields and depending on their interests and capabilities, they are being given the opportunity to work in the family business.

Whether a daughter will eventually succeed the patriarch (in cases where there is no male heir or he is not interested in joining the family business), is a question to which there is no uniform answer. Each business and its management needs; each business family and its socio-cultural environment and each female candidate for succession - will have their own characteristics influencing the eventual outcome - one way or the other. But, the emergence of successful women entrepreneurs and corporate executives in India (as well as the success of Indian born women executives abroad), has definitely helped generate more ambition and confidence among young women aspiring for top positions within the family businesses as well as outside.

References :

1. The Family Business Answer Book (quoted earlier)
2. Mrs. Anu Aga, Chairman Emeritus, Thermax Ltd.
3. Ms. Shefali Munjal, Hero Group, Hindustan Times, 23.9,06.
4. Dr. Gita Piramal, Corporate Historian, Hindustan Times, 23.9.06.

CASE 6

NEW CORPORATE INITIATIVES IN INDIAN AGRICULTURE

Dr R Singh
NMIMS University, Mumbai, India.

Abstract

Vertical coordination is common in agriculture. In India due to legal restrictions on contract farming, this is a relatively new area of research, especially when the government is toying with the idea of bringing out legislative changes to facilitate contract farming and vertical co-ordination in agriculture. Indian corporate and rural India has entered into collaborative partnership through vertical co-ordination. The common thread among all these initiates have been integrating and tightening the supply chain. Mahindra's Shubhlabh service rallies Kisan Kendra, ITC e-Chaupal, and Kisan India.com are new agribusiness models, which are based on vertical co-ordination between Indian corporate and Indian farmer.This case paper evaluates three such attempts by corporate India i.e., PepsiCo's contract farming in Punjab, ITC's e-Chaupal and Mahindra Shubhlabh services.

Introduction

The Government of India new agricultural policy envisages that "private sector participation will be promoted through contract farming and land leasing agreements to allow accelerated technology transfer, capital inflows and assured market for crop production, especially of oilseeds, cotton and horticultural crop", following this announcement a number of innovative agribusiness models have come up. Indian corporate and rural India has entered into collaborative partnership through vertical co-ordination. The common thread among all these initiates have been integrating and tightening the supply chain. Mahindra's Shubhlabh service rallies Kisan Kendra, ITC e-Chaupal, and Kisan India.com are new agribusiness models, which are based on vertical co-ordination between Indian corporate and Indian farmer.

This vertical coordination is supposed to eliminate the inefficiencies in agricultural marketing which arises due to multi-layer intermediaries sucking away a large chunk of the margins and leaving nothing for the farmer on the one hand and lack of basic availability of infrastructure as well as technology on the other.

These vertical coordination models are common in agriculture worldwide. In India, land ceiling laws limited such vertical coordination. Corporate farming, captive farming or contract farming were only allowed in plantations, degraded or waste lands and so on. With the government's change in heart regarding contract farming, a stage is set for such vertical coordination in Indian agriculture. This case evaluates three such attempts by corporate India i.e., PepsiCo's contract farming in Punjab, ITC's e-Chaupal and Mahindra Shubhlabh services.

PepsiCo contract farming

Vertical co-ordination has emerged as a viable model for food processing industry as well as agri-commodity markets in India. These firms face problems of regular supplies and also face the risk of poor quality products. The new structure in agribusiness supply chain is to move away from deals to relationship. Neither buyer nor vendor can take each other for granted. Relationships are becoming mutually independent. Firms are contracting to farmers to plant the contractor's crop on his land. Farmer harvests and delivers to the firm, a quantum of produce, based upon anticipated yield and contracted acreage. This is at a pre-agreed price. The relationship between firms can take any form, just a deal to buy the produce to one where lots of cost sharing and support are provided to the farmers. In the Indian context despite a restriction on contract farming some exception were provided to firm on case-to-case basis.

Like farmers all over the world, Indian farmers too are happy with existing contract farming arrangement in the country. Hindustan Lever Limited, Nijjer and Pepsi are involved in contracts, where tomato, potato and chillies are procured under contracts and processed into value added food products for domestic and export markets. Market fed a farmer's co-operative in Punjab, is engaged in contract farming in mustard. Rallis and HLL are into wheat, Dynamix dairy in milk, ACE in floriculture and horticulture. Number of firms engaged in contract farming is increasing everyday.

However, the company has sold off its tomato plant to HLL since tomatoes were not fitting into Pepsi's export oriented policies. It is still into machine intensive nursery operations. It has almost wrapped up chillies and its tomato operating is limited by the extent to which it buys from the contracted farms and open market. In fact, as of now, Pepsi is concentrating on Basmati and other varieties of rice.

As a part of our research we still thought of studying PepsiCo foray into contract farming which brought about a revolution in Sangrur, district of Punjab. Let's look at the initial experiment.

PepsiCo has done a wonderful job in Sangrur, district of Punjab. Farmers are expected to harvest and deliver to the contractor, a quantum of produce, based upon anticipated yield at an agreed price. Towards these ends, farmers may or may not supply the farmer with selected inputs. But, Pepsi went a step further and in their contract-farming model they involved farmer as a partner. Their model actually is a mix of technology transfer of an integrated spectrum of horticultural services with a focus on farmer economics and competing crops.

Pepsi collaborated with Punjab Agricultural University who provided the knowledge of horticulture with special focus on Punjab. Punjab agro Industries Corporation provided the extension support and PepsiCo pooled in its international research experience and marketing and commercial skills. This partnership led towards the building block of the business. There were three component of the building block, they are, R and D activities, Technology transfer and commercialization of agriculture. A core team of scientists and research specialists were assembled. Punjab Agriculture University seconded key personnel to the project i.e., a vegetable breeder, a soil scientist, a plant pathologist, an agronomist and an entomologist. PepsiCo provided the full-time services of three overseas consultants-experts on the growing of tomato and Frito-Lay expertise on potato. Infrastructure and facilities for R and D activities were put in place. There is evaluation of varieties from sources in the world; they are then adapted to local conditions. Extension personnel are selected from among the farmers themselves. They are responsible for the contact with the farmers; they help in diffusion of technology from lab to field. They use various means of communication to disseminate knowledge and monitor crops from nursery to procurement.

Farmers find help in terms of land preparation, crop monitoring during growing period. Help in terms of harvesting, transportation and logistics. Finally, farmers are paid promptly and the agreed price. The net impact of this was dramatic; Tomato yields increased dramatically from 16 to 52 MT per hectares. With increase in productivity prices of these crops declined but farm incomes increased by more than 2.5 times. This happened after three years. Contract farming transformed the economy of Sangrur and exposed them to world class farming, as well as remunerative and assured market.

This was the company well thought out relationship building exercise with their suppliers. Literatures on supplier buyer relationships are proof enough that relationship centered business models bring very high incremental operating margins. PepsiCo gained by receiving uninterrupted and regular flow of quality raw materials. Protection from fluctuations in market pricing they could plan for the long run. This experiment in corporate farming led to long run commitment and hence assured Pepsi of a dedicated supplier base. PepsiCo generated good will for itself. Sadly, PepsiCo has sold off its tomato operations to HLL; PepsiCo was finding Tomato contract farming difficult to operate due to archaic tax laws and its export operations become unsustainable and not profitable.

Looking critically at the model, we conclude that, Pepsi's model is a better model of contract farming as compared to HLL and Nijjer. According to a study, carried out by Sukhpal Singh (2001) which evaluated Pepsi, Nijjer and HLL contract-farming practices, farmers on the whole agree that contract farming benefits them, they were happy about the contract system. Even these firms have been beneficiary of contract-farming in terms of assured supplies. However, this study detected various operational problems in the functioning of these contract-farming practices. The farmers' reported problems like poor technical assistance, delayed payments and outright cheating in dealing and manipulation of norms by the firms. HLL and Nijjer have not fulfilled their commitment of buying farms produce at agreed price and quantity. Farmers had little bargaining power with the company; both these firms pass on the risk to farmers. Both company had market specification contracts and not production management or resource provision contracts. In the event of company not meeting its fulfillment the legal protection was not available to the farmers, as contract farming is not allowed in India.

The same farmers rated PepsiCo experiments with contract farming a better model; number of farmers unhappy was marginal in case of PepsiCo as compared to Nijjer and HLL.

But in the larger sense, PepsiCo has treated farmers as their supply base and had worked only with the intention of creating sustainable supply bases. As the acreage under tomato crop increase and production too increases the open market prices is going to fall and then company bases its contract price on the basis of this open market price. Farmers in Sangrur, as well as Ganganagar, smell foul, as Pepsi has started paying them as low a price as Rs.1.50. At times, as reported in Dainik Bhaskar (2nd September, 2000), they have also failed to fulfill their contract.

The only advice to PepsiCo is that such a wonderful agreement can go haywire if they do not learn to care for their suppliers. First PepsiCo must learn to fulfill commitments and enter into an option contracts with the farmers group, i.e. When the open market prices are higher than the contract price, they should buy at open market price and vice-versa. They should learn from the experiences of HLL that contract-farming without building mutual trust with supply chain partners might be dangerous for the company itself. PepsiCo should treat farmers as partners and pass them some of the benefits to create a long-lasting and sustainable relationship for a sustainable business. No collaborative experiment of this kind can succeed unless PepsiCo start working on common interest of farmers and it self. There must be openness between farmers group and Pepsi. Pepsi also needs to share its benefits to create the right kind of trust with the farmers.

Doing things the old way, by showing natural resistance to change, resorting to betrayal for its benefit, by lying, misleading, misrepresenting and exhibiting inconsistency in behavioral attitudes can lead the way towards the failure of collaborations.

Instead of trying to squeeze the farmers of some surplus, as suggested by HLL chief Banga, firms need to collaborate to reduce the facility cost of a service center which can help input firms to manage their demand and customer better and help food processing industries to source timely and quality supplies. Its time that Indian firms partner with Indian farmer to bring about an agricultural revolution which will lead to a win-win situation both for the farmers and firms.

Mahindra Shubhlabh

A wholly-owned subsidiary of tractor major, Mahindra Shubhlabh came into existence to provide total farm solution to the Indian farmers. There were two aspects to the business, one was the commodity trading and second one was to provide one stop shop to the farmers for all his needs. This is like providing total solution to almost all the problems of Indian farmers. The constituent of the Shubhlabh model was to provide: (1) Arrange all agri-inputs such as seeds, fertilizers, and pesticides and so on to farmer, (2) Rent out farm machinery like tractors, transplanters and other special machinery that helps to reduce the cost to the farmer, (3) Provide commercial agricultural extension by bi-weekly visits to the farms, (4) Offer crop spraying, harvesting and post harvesting services, and (5) Provide commodity trading in final produce of the farmers. Initially these both aspects of business were supposed to be highly IT driven. Based on a white paper by McKinsey, Mahindra and Mahindra identified provision of total farm solution to Indian farmers a great opportunity. Both commodity and farm solution were supposed to be highly Information Technology driven models.

In order to increase its reach to remote off villages, it adopted a hub and spoke model.

The first total farm solution shop was opened by MSSL in Madurai. Tamil Nadu was favoured to other states as spill over effects, in case of a problem, were expected to be less. It was also an ideal selection because MSSL wanted to begin its work in paddy. Mammoth investments were made at Madurai (the first center). The super market for farmers should have a good area, a place in the outskirt of Madurai was identified, some material placed. Tie-up with the input companies was not difficult on account of the Mahindra brand name and the fact that this was an experiment. Investment in IT was also made.

Initially, hub and the spokes were to be operated with the help of franchises. Franchises were expected to make huge investments, and pay a non-refundable sign up fees. Franchises were to reach the villages. The initials model's project was approximately 1 crore rupees. This included almost everything, the cost of property, equipments, land for carrying out agri R&D, computers, tractors, other implements, office space and working capital required. The sign-up fees were rupees 5 lakhs. This fee was non refundable. Mahindra also had had to invest to set up systems and procedures. Mahindra expected a lot to sign up by prospective dealers (franchises), the belief was that the franchises was getting (1) definite sale through registered farmers, and also the products recommended by Mahindra's for farming. They were obviously of high quality and had relatively better margins. (2) Money will be made through farm consultancy fee that the farmers will pay. (3) The franchises were getting the distributorship of sorts of various companies in one shot without paying deposits. (4) The franchisee would earn money through equipment rental.

Theoretically, this sounds fine and McKinsey, which was the architect of this model, seems to be totally swayed away by models of total farm solution operating in western economies. It ignored the ground realities of the Indian agricultural economy. The non-refundable sign-up fees came as a major stumbling block, most dealers in agri-input industry have to give only security deposits against which they either get a fixed deposit interest or get materials worth that amount immediately. Many of the dealers, which had the capability to invest, were already one-stop shop themselves dealing with a whole host of input companies as distributors, giving farmers advice informally from their shops and doing farming themselves. They also had field assistants and contract employees from companies like BASF, Bayer and other agrochemical majors who do field trials demonstration too.

The input industry is a highly credit driven industry. The credit given in this industry is quite high and often span from 90 days to 180 days. The dealers rotate five lakhs and can do a business worth a crore. Any new business model should provide that opportunity. MSSL seems to be adamant and their belief that they were creating value for the franchises played havoc with their business model. Instead of educating and developing dealers they relied on their brand equity and were taken aback when there was not a single sign up in the first phase. In just eight months the sign up fees was brought down to 4.7 lakhs. During the same period IT model was abandoned, as they realized that franchises viewed it as a useless investment. The new young and dynamic team recruited by MSSL could not make this model work. After two years MSSL was at around 5 to 8 per cent of its projected revenue. Only five centers were operational against the projected forty.

In the third year of its existence, in e-agri commodity trading,where nothing was going right was shut down. Employees adjusted in one stop shop. Even the separate offices were shut down and the staff was told to share the offices of Mahindra and Mahindra tractors. With the lowering of the project costs at the end of the third year, there were around 12 centers operating. Four of them were joint ventures in Kota, Madurai, Miralguda and one more. There were around 8 sign-ups in all and turnover was around Rs.6 crores. It had a total manpower of 65.

At the end of the third year, the business model was redefined once again. MSSL brought down the sign up fee from Rs.5 lakhs to Rs.3 lakhs. Project cost was brought down from 47 lakhs to 27 lakhs; with an inbuilt flexibility of it being brought down further to facilitate new sign-ups.

Having shut e-agri, the fund released was used for business development of MSSL. The company expanded again to other territories viz., Gujarat, Madhya Pradesh, Maharashtra and Chattisgarh. While these sign-ups were taking place, the old centers with higher investments were expecting high services and were getting impatient. This led to many legal cases and closures of centers. The model was tinkered once again and the sign-up fees were brought down to Rs.1 lakh and that, too, it was refundable. The sub franchises were given only one tehsil as against one district earlier. The number increases on one hand closures too increase on other.

In the meantime, the IFC funding of Rs.11 crores has come at the right time. This funding with its well-laid conditions may not be sufficient. Top management continues to be impatient, employees continue to quit and franchises appointment with loan guarantee still remains tough. Farmer's appreciation of farm solution and the entire process is poor.

e-Chaupal

ITC started its ambitious e-Chaupal project with an intention of enhancing the global competitiveness of Indian agriculture and raising the standard of living in Indian villages. It intends to leverage information technology to reduce aggregate cost of its value chain and to extract value through a near disinter-mediation of the supply chain. It is a well-known fact that the sheer number of intermediaries in food and agricultural chain are too many making chain uncompetitive as well as these intermediaries block market information making transaction cost unfavorable to the Indian farmer. With this e-initiative ITC hopes to disintermediate the supply chain through virtual integration.

ITC is of the firm belief that intermediaries who yield substantial socio-political power in their belt cannot be totally eliminated. But they could be disassociated from the intermediation of the information flows. Taking this understanding as the basis they have structured the e-Chaupal initiative.

How does the e-Chaupal operate? Across various villages in interior Madhya Pradesh, Karnataka, Uttar Pradesh and Andhra Pradesh ITC's e-Chaupal's holding Internet-enabled Pentium desktops and printers display the itcibd.com portal. These Internet kiosks are manned by a lead farmer of the village, called the Sanchalaks. The Sanchalak is trained to operate the computer. These Sanchalaks, with the help of Internet kiosks are supposed to perform three distinct activities; (1) Information and knowledge dissemination: These kiosks display real-time data on market price prevailing in the Mandis across States. They also carry information on weather and have a knowledge bank of best scientific practices. (2) Virtual aggregation of demand and supply: By aggregating both buyers and sellers ITC intends to reduce the aggregate cost by providing a kind of commodity exchange which disassociates intermediaries from intermediation of information flow making the chain more competitive. (3) Allowing retailing of agri-inputs as well as other products and services.

The e-Chaupals provide ITC with the opportunity to directly purchase soya, rice and other crop from the farmers. This has, no doubt, provided the farmers with alternative route to Mandi through online access and transaction across remote locations. This has reduced transaction cost pre- and post-Chaupal experiment. Farmers incur transaction cost, which arose due to trolley freight to Mandi, labour cost, cost of labour khadi karnai and handling cost. Process incurs commission to agents, cost of gunny bags, and loading cost of labour freight and transit loss cost. Both farmer and process transaction cost works against the interest of farmers and the company. With the help of e-Chaupal, ITC has been able to reduce this transaction cost drastically claiming a win–win situation for both farmers as well as itself. The coverage of e-Chaupal is currently around 3,50,000 farmers growing soyabean, coffee, wheat, rice, pulses and shrimp in around 3,50,000 villages through 650 kiosks across four States. (ET).

What about Information and knowledge dissemination? What is the advantage of these kiosks? A study done by us on strategic assessments of information portals in agriculture brings out the fact that these portals were very poor in terms both reach and richness. The trade off between richness and reach determines the ability to tap strategic gains. Reach simply means the number of people at home or at work exchanging information. Richness is defined by three aspects of the information. The first is the bandwidth, or the amount of information that can be moved from sender to receiver in a given time. The second aspect is degree to which the information can be customized. The third aspect is interactivity, dialogue is possible for a small group, but to reach millions of people the message must be a monologue. The communication of the information to a large audience has acquired compromises in bandwidth, customization and interactivity. When companies conduct business with each another, the number of parties they deal with is inversely proportional to the richness of the information they need to exchange.

Reach is critical for any Internet based alternative to work in a diversified agricultural economy in India. Has ITC been able to connect these diversifies agroclimatic zones with kiosks? ITC experiment is truly held by many as Information technology revolution connecting remote villages of this country.

In order to make a first-hand assessment of these portals we took MP as a case study. In order to provide all the services ITC has invested close to around Rs.2.5 to 3 lakhs at each Chaupal where VSAT is required and an investment of Rs.75,000 to Rs.1,00,000 at other places. They have done extensive work on data connectivity from the existing telephone exchanges and have worked with BSNL to upgrade their exchanges. Approx. 500 nodes have been set up across MP of which 100 are connected with VSATs. The Investment seems to serve two purposes, one to provide information to farmers and two, to provide infrastructure for the transaction processing system which will capture expected and actual sales, stocks, customer orders on input side and the produce information on the output side.

ITC has done a commendable job of connecting the remote of villages with the help of Internet kiosks. Reach is commendable. But the richness of this initiative comes under some shadow of doubts. They do not provide any other information for the farmers except weather information, which they get by collaborating with the IMD. As far as Mandi prices in nearby Mandi are concerned, it is quite useful and farmers know much before moving out of his village what price is he going to get and which Mandi should he sell in. Sanchalaks do the grading for the farmers and also provide this information. But do all Sanchalaks and all Chaupals provide this information? Of the four Chaupals we visited, two were active and were doing business both on soya purchase and retail sales as well as information dissemination. Of the other two, third one was soya purchase but did not appear very active on information dissemination front and the fourth one was never operationalised.

While examining these portals, we found that the portal did not have the requisite richness for it to become information and knowledge dissemination kiosk. The information as regards to best practices, integrated crop production, inputs fertilizer and seeds were of poor quality. Information was not customized to the farming needs of these agro climatic regions. It seems ITC was only interested in procuring supply for its International business division needs. It has not been able to enhance the richness of its portal and serve its customer better. In all these villages the only information disseminated was the prices and weather conditions. As regards to selling pesticides and fertilizers and seeds to farmers in the villages via Sanchalaks was and is in doubt as it clearly is in conflict with the traditional channels which is purely based on a push system. ITC has not taken care to see that there is an amicable acceptability of input trading by its Chaupals. Most decision to trade input of another company does not take local socioeconomic and business reality into account. The partnerships between these companies are almost absent. Most farmers did not agree with ITC claim that farmers have been getting better prices for their produce is also countered by some of the farmers who believe except for minor benefits like de-bagging expenses etc. Farmers also said that the company does not pay the price agreed by the Sanchalaks. Sometimes, grading is downgraded and hence the net farmers realization. The significant advantage which farmer has gained is right weight, which was a major worry in traditional Mandi.

The way ahead

Agri-initiatives taken by Indian corporates will play an important role in dissemination of right information as well as knowledge, provide total farm solution and act as buyer of agri-produce as well as provide the resource for producing these agri-produce. These firms have to strive hard to create a win-win situation both for themselves as well as the farmer. A well thought out collaborative model could help firms share facility and infrastructure cost on one hand and increase complementarities in their marketing efforts enhancing customer satisfaction through a partnered customer relationship management approach.

The Three firms can use their resources and can very well form a collaborative agri-service center. The proposed model has collaboration and partnership as the basis. This partnership culminates into formation of farmer service center. Farmer service center would be run as a private enterprise between the food processor and a number of other input providers such as bank, agrochemical/seed/fertilizer, farm equipment manufacturers, and so, on. Either the agri-input provider or food processor can take the lead in establishing this model. The benefit of this model is very significant. Agri-input would be made available to the farmer directly to the farmer at cheaper rates. Credit and insurance would be available to the farmer. The farmer service center would provide extension services. The food processor would access the farm producer directly. Specialized grain-handling equipment, transport and vertical storage would be installed reducing both costs spillage losses to pests. Such a model will drive down the cost of agricultural produce. The farmer's efficiencies would result in increased production and increased off take, and increase his incomes, despite lower prices. Indeed a win-win situation for both farmers and consumers.

Questions:

1. Compare the business models adopted by The three firms to tackle their supply chain problems.
2. What are the flaws in the existing Agricultural supply chain?
3. Can Collaboration between various Initiatives in rural markets solve the problem of scale and make business models more sustainable?

References:

- Sukhpal Singh (2001), "Contract Farming in Indian Agriculture" IIAE, October - December, 2001.
- Economic Times "Rural Economy" CD rom 2004.

CASE 7

MTNL AT A CROSSROAD

R M Chaturvedi
MTNL, Mumbai, India

Abstract

This case shows how an Indian Public Sector undertaking (read Mahanagar Telephone Nigam Limited-MTNL) in telecom sector, which enjoyed a 100% monopoly over the market, responded to the competitive forces when Globalization, Privatization and Liberalization hit the market and economy in post-1990 period. The Public Sector Undertaking (PSU) had to gear up to face the competition. From its routine management working, it had to change itself and that too fast before the private players capture the market. The case deals with the various roadblocks and bottlenecks, a PSU normally faces because generally the people in the system resist to change the old system, as they are comfortable working in it. The case brings out various changes, strategic initiatives and other steps taken to meet the challenges posed by the competition. While the company has till now handled the competition well, recently there has been a spurt in aggressiveness from competitors, and it is once again at a point where further and tougher decisions need to be taken to survive the market forces. The case also provides a sound understanding of Telecom Industry which is not only playing a important role, and growing at a fast pace but also passing through a highly dynamic and turbulent phase. Prevalent price wars while a boon to customers are forcing companies to work in a highly efficient manner, constantly adjusting their strategy to respond to market, customer and regulatory requirements

Introduction

Sitting in the car on his way back home after attending the management meeting which developed into an intense brain storming session, Mr. Gopalan, Chief General Manager, MTNL was reflecting on the proceedings that took place. Mr. Gopalan was more concerned as he is one of the most prospective candidates to become the Executive Director of MTNL in the near future. The meeting had a heated debate about the strategy and pricing policy to be followed by MTNL in view of the increased aggressiveness on the part of its competitors who are willing to slash the rates to any extent to get the customers. He was concerned as no consensus could be reached in the meeting. It was an awkward feeling for him to get adjusted to the continuously changing scenario with ever increasing expectations on the part of customers and willingness to do anything for profitable customers on the part of competitors. He had to come out with constructive, innovative and competitive offerings to its customers to retain them. As he reclined back relaxing on the back seat of his car, he tried to analyze the Indian Telecom Industry's role played by MTNL till now and how MTNL could fit in the present scenario.

To get a better and comprehensive understanding of the changing business environment Mr. Gopalan arranged for a presentation and write up by his Business Analysis Group headed by Mr. Raman, Head of Business Development (BD) Unit. He also invited his senior management team and members of Management Committee to attend the same with a view to arrive at certain guidelines and decisions to forge further strategy to the handle present situation.

Salient Points of write up presented by Mr. Raman to the Management Committee are placed below.

Origin of Telecommunication

Telecommunication has come a long way since the invention of "electrical speech machine", now called Telephone, in 1876 by Dr. Alexander Graham Bell. Now, it has been a well established fact that an efficient and well developed communications system is a basic requirement in any modern industrialized economy. The saying "If trade is the life of an economy then telecommunications can truly be regarded as the nervous system of both the economy and society" shows the importance of telecommunication in modern times.

Telecommunication in India was introduced at the same time as in other more advanced parts of the world. Mahanagar Telephone Nigam Limited (MTNL) is one of the two, Government owned company providing telecommunication services presently in India.

Brief History of Indian Telecom

In India, 1851 was the year when the first telecommunication line was opened for traffic for official work only. For public usage, the telegraph services were available in 1855. Subsequently, India saw its first telephone exchange in 1882 in Bombay.

Fast forwarding to post-Independence, until the mid-1980s, the telecommunications sector in India was a monopoly controlled by the Government of India (GOI) through the Department of Posts and Telegraphs of the Ministry of Communications, providing all telecommunications services, both domestic and international. The Indian Telegraph Act of 1885 established the GOI's monopoly in the sector and, together with the Indian Wireless Telegraphy Act of 1933, provided the legal framework for the regulation of the Indian telecommunications industry.

However, in the mid-1980s, faced with rapidly increasing demand for telecommunications services and equipment, the GOI commenced reorganization of the sector designed to facilitate the rapid introduction of new technology, stimulate the growth of the telecommunications industry and tap the resources of the private sector in facilitating such technological innovation and growth. The reorganization included the division of the Department of Posts and Telegraphs into the Department of Telecommunication (DOT) and the Department of Posts in January 1985. As a continuem to this process of restructuring, a need was felt to set up a separate organization for providing communication facilities to large metro cities. This was how MTNL came into existence in 1986.

Major Phases of Indian Telecom Industry

As the world realized the importance of telecommunication infrastructure for overall growth of economy, there was a move to enhance the telecommunication infrastructure and ensure availability of telecommunication facilities at all places and at an affordable price.

In the post-1991 era of liberalization, Policy makers of India realized the importance of telecommunication infrastructure for over all growth of economy and there was a move to enhance the telecommunication infrastructure and ensure availability of telecommunication facilities at all places and at an affordable price. It has been said that 1% increase in telephone density leads to a 3% increase in Gross Domestic Product (GDP). To achieve this kind of economic and growth objectives there was a wave to privatize and liberalize telecom industry in a regulated manner and GOI clearly declared its intentions to privatize and liberalize the industry through the National Telecommunication Policy 1994 (NTP 1994) announced in May, 1994. To implement this policy, licenses for cellular mobiles for four metros were issued in November 1994 and Letter of Intent (LOI) for basic services was issued in October 1996. Due to these developments, MTNL had to gear itself to meet the challenges posed by competition.

During recent past, despite of all the regulatory constraints, telecom industry has been growing at fast pace. The mobile sector has grown from around 10 million subscribers in 2002 to more than 142 million by December 2006. Whilst Global System for Mobile Communication (GSM) technology still dominates and stands at 105.4 million (Dec'2006)[1], Code Division Multiple Access (CDMA) with 36.7 million (Dec'2006)[2] subscribers has quickly grabbed around 25% of the market. The mobile industry should continue to boom. Fixed-line services grew strongly for a while but have been experiencing near zero growth of late, primarily due to surrender experienced in landline connection.

Study of MTNL or for that matter of Indian Telecommunication can be divided into following phases:

---

[1] *Source: http://www.coai.in*

[2] *Source: http://www.telegeography.com*

- First phase continued from 1947 to 1997: during which telecommunication was a monopoly of the GOI, and due to various constraints, the demands were not fully met. The industry was operating in a sellers market.
- Second Phase: Between 1995 and 1998: During this phase gradually competition got introduced .
- Third Phase1998-2006: the industry had to function in a stiff competitive environment.
- 2006 onwards: The competition grew more aggressive, as operators matured and FDI limits in telecom sector was increased.

In this case study, we would be dwelling more on the post-1998 scenario and on the telecom needs of the corporate segment, those who pay higher revenue.[3]

MTNL History

MTNL was set up on 1st April 1986 by the Government of India, holding 56.25% stake in the company, to upgrade the quality of telecom services, expand the telecom network, introduce new services, and to raise revenue for telecom development needs of India's key metros – Delhi, the political capital and Mumbai, the business capital of India. In the past 20 years, the company has taken rapid strides to emerge as India's leading and one of Asia's largest telecom operating companies. Besides having a strong financial base, by this time MTNL has achieved a market share of approximately 15% of the Indian telecommunication network with a customer base of over 5.92 million lines. The company has also been in the forefront of technology induction by converting 100% of its telephone exchange network into state-of-the-art digital mode.

MTNL's Mission, Vision and Objectives

Mission:

To remain market leader in providing world- class telecom IT related services and to become a global player

Vision:

Become a total solution provider company and to provide world-class telecom service at affordable price.

Become a global telecom company and to find place in the 'Fortune 500' companies.

Enter into and expand new services viz. long distances, cellular mobile, Internet and IN services and development of telecom softwaware.

Become the largest provider of private networks and leased lines.

Venture into other areas in India and abroad on the strength of its core competency.

---

[3] *The case is prepared as a basis for discussion for academic purpose only. Names bear no resemblance to reality. Data given is approximately accurate for the purpose of analysis.*

Corporate Objectives

To provide latest technology and services to customers.

To achieve the highest level of customer satisfaction and delight.

To fund R&D projects which will help MTNL in introducing technology, understanding customer needs, trying out and indigenizing new technologies.

To diversify in other areas for providing telecom services at national and international levels.

To provide convergence of Telecom, Information Technology and related services.

To improve productivity by training and redeployment of manpower.

To work for social benefits.

MTNL Performance: Pre - 1998 (Before active Competition)

Performance of MTNL from its inception to 1997 is given at Table 1

Table 1 MTNL OVERALL PERFORMANCE1987-1997 (Rs. in Million)											
	1987	**1988**	**1989**	**1990**	**1991**	**1992**	**1993**	**1994**	**1995**	**1996**	**1997**
Revenue	5410	7230	10470	11720	13180	15730	18740	25217	30540	35186	40961
Capital Investment	1910	2910	3900	5250	5580	6130	6410	8370	9980	9840	8850
Profit Before Tax (PBT)	**1370**	**2060**	**3920**	**4230**	**3540**	**4290**	**4650**	**7804**	**9791**	**12480**	**14821**
Fixed Assets	9790	12040	15060	18060	23150	28860	33510	42025	49115	59017	69873
Total DELs(in thousands)	845	941	1018	1111	1220	1397	1587	1850	2208	2610	3012
Revenue in Rs. Per DEL	6405	7680	10287	10546	10806	11264	11807	13634	13835	13482	13598

Source: *MTNL Annual Reports 1986-97 and Various MTNL Annual Magazines*

MTNL Telecom Environment (Post-1998)

MTNL being an incumbent telecom service provider had 100% market share at the beginning of competition phase and could dictate service terms and prices to a large extent. MTNL was primarily into the business of providing landlines for which it has developed huge infrastructure in terms of telephone exchanges and a large network of copper cables. Huge capital and infrastructure requirement for landline, provide a strong entry barrier to other telecom companies in this segment. Landline services are the highest contributor to the company's revenue.

However, with the introduction of alternate disruptive technologies of mobile telephones, competitors are able to roll out mobile networks at a much faster pace. As the mobile technology requires just installation of few central exchanges and antennas around the city, the roll out is much faster. Further, as the mobile instrument is to be purchased by the customer, this component of cost is transferred from service provider to customers and in turn, there is huge reduction in capital cost involved. Due to reduction in infrastructure cost involved per line, the services can be provided at reduced rates in comparison to landline telephones. While the clarity of the speech may not be as good as landline, convenient features of mobile instruments and facility of communication while on move has made mobile communication a preferred mode of communication service.

As the competition increased and subsequently with the approval of the Foreign Direct Investment (FDI) increase to 74% from 49%, there was large entry of foreign investors and with their long experience of handling competition and their huge financial strength brought in a new dimension to the ongoing fierce competition. Gradually, higher preemptive infrastructure investment was becoming the norm of the day, as an outcome the market share of MTNL was bound to come down and it did. However, due to increasing awareness, advertising activities of the new service providers and easy availability of telecommunication facilities, market expanded and there was enough place for everyone to grow. Nevertheless, MTNL had to make changes to give higher importance to customers and make provision of services easier, which MTNL did. Despite this, MTNL is losing its growth potential and customer base, not only to its competitors in the landline segment, but also to mobile segment.

During the competition phase, between 1998 and 2006, MTNL has taken several steps in the areas of technology up gradation, strategic initiatives, customer services, HR practices, operations and image building, to maintain it as a profit making and growing organization. Through these initiatives, recognizing and leveraging its strength and underplaying its weakness, MTNL has posed a tough challenge for the competitors. Claims and projections of private operators that they will be able to take advantage of the weaknesses of Government system and will be able to capture the market easily have not yet come true.

MTNL's Initiatives to Challenge Competition

Below are some of the initiatives taken up by MTNL in the recent years to fight competition and serve the customers needs and requirements efficiently:

(A) Technology Up Gradation

- Made all its telephone exchanges digital and added new technology exchanges.

(B) Strategic Initiatives

- Leveraging on its core competency i.e. copper lines, serving not only voice but offering Assymetric Digital Subscriber Line (ADSL 2+) broadband, Games on Demand, Internet Protocol Television (IPTV) solution etc on copper line.

(Pic 1: OCB-283 Digital Exchange of MTNL – upgrading Technology)

- Organizational restructuring to handle competition by setting up of independent units viz. Business Development, Corporate Accounts Management, Sales and Marketing unit.
- International Operations *(See Operations of MTNL in the later part of this case).*

(C) Improved Customer Interface

- By setting up Quick Customer Service Centers (QCSC), Brand promotion and Image Handling, e-interaction etc

(D) Re-Defined Operations and Procedures

- Streamlining and simplifying operational procedures.
- Enhancing Customer Friendliness and Responsiveness.
- Rolling out new services like internet service, mobile service, broadband bundled with IPTV and games on demand, Launching Wireless Fidelity (Wi-Fi) services, National Long Distance (NLD) service etc. Wireless interoperability for Microwave Access (Wi-Max), and International Long Distance service are planned to be launched shortly.

- Automation and Computerization Initiatives viz. Fault Reporting System (FRS), Customer Services Management System (CSMS), Network Management System (NMS), Bill Presentment and Payment System (BPPS), Fraud Management and Control Centre (FMCC), along with other standard systems used in large enterprises.
- Repair Centre at Regional and National level along with Telecom Control and Management Information System (TCMIS), to provide control and monitoring of the whole exchange network and to reduce dependency on external vendors for PCB level repairs of Exchange Cards.

(E) Improved Human Resource Practices through

- Employee training programs.
- Right Sizing its employees strength through offering Voluntary Retirement Schemes and recruitment of qualified engineers, chartered accountants and MBAs (Master in Business Administration).
- Setting up of Centre for Excellence in Telecom Technology and Management (CETTM), a certified ISO: 9001-2000 training centre.

(Pic 2: MTNL Training Centre- CETTM)

MTNL STAKEHOLDERS AND INFLUENCERS

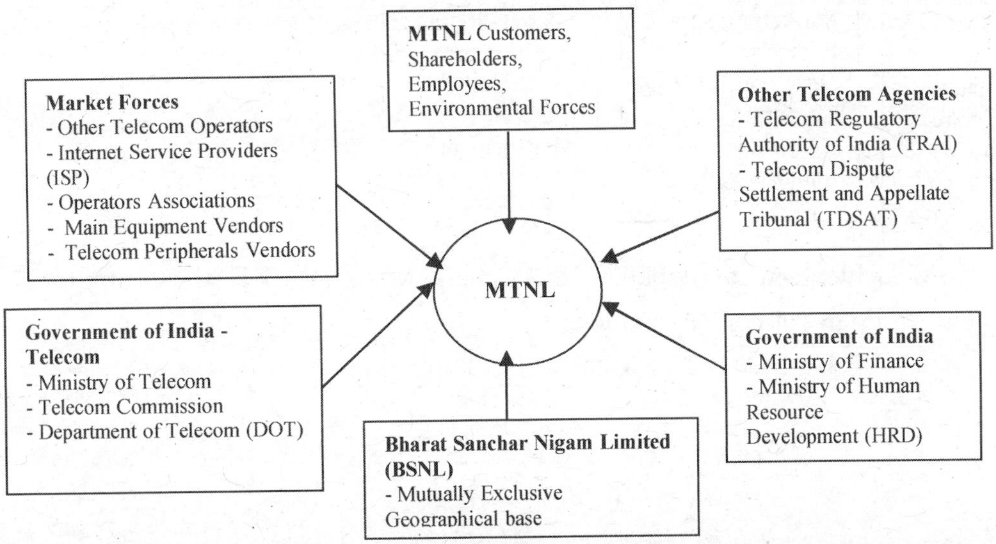

ORGANISATIONAL CHART

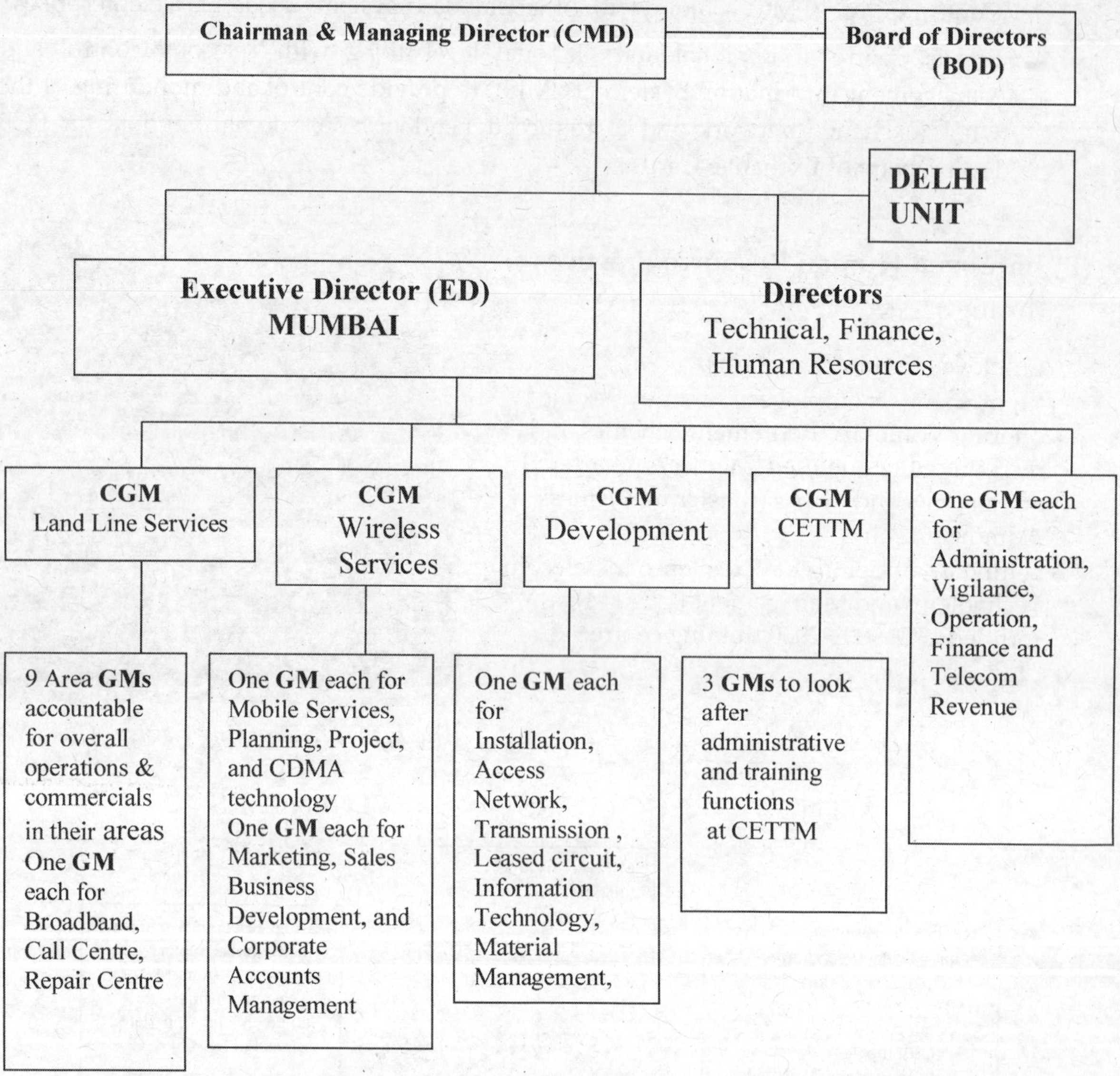

CGM – Chief General Manager, GM- General Manager, CETTM – Centre for Excellence in Telecom Technology.

Human Resources in MTNL

Most of the employees of MTNL belonged to Government sector with high salaries in comparison to market, especially for lower cadres where number of employees is high. MTNL being a Public Sector Undertaking (PSU), has to comply with relatively stringent employment criteria and hence per employee cost, including perks and overheads, of MTNL is much higher than market cost.

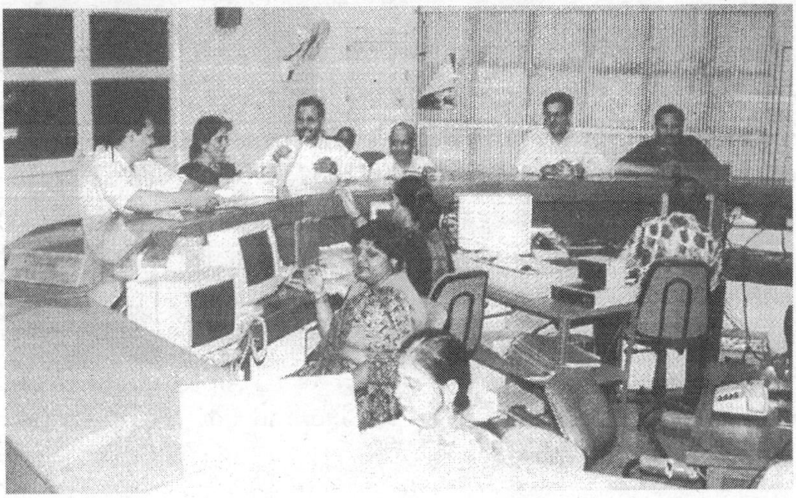

(Pic 3: MTNL employees interacting with Customers)

On Formation of MTNL, all the employees who were working in the specified geographic reason continued to work for MTNL on deputation basis. Subsequently most of the employees agreed to forgo their GOI employee's status in favor of becoming MTNL employees through a process of absorption which entitled them better salary structure. However, senior officers who were part of Indian Telecommunication Services (ITS) preferred to continue as GOI employees primarily because of pensionary benefits guaranteed by GOI, even though the salary structure of MTNL is marginally better. MTNL management made serious attempts, including allegedly pressure tactics, to get such employees absorbed into MTNL. However these employees continue to be Govt. of India, employees with the liability of being transferred to anywhere in India in departments working under Ministry of Communication.

Customer Segmentation:

In terms of volume of traffic generated and number of lines utilized, customers could be categorized as corporate customers, enterprise customers, Small and Medium Enterprises (SME) segment and individual customers. On the basis of revenue generated, the customers could be categorized low revenue (rental only), mid revenue and high revenue customers. There could be other categorization based on demographics, behavioural and other preferences as teenagers, office goers, housewives and senior citizens.

Product Segmentation

MTNL offers most of the telecommunication services starting from traditional Land Line to Wi-Fi Services. Land line telephone has since been the major source of revenue generation for MTNL. It has ventured into Mobile segment Viz. Global Standard for Mobile (GSM) in 2000 and CDMA technology in 2004 to ensure that it is present in both the mobile service segment. In addition to the traditional Internet-dial-up service, MTNL launched Broadband services in 2004, which has been subscribed by more than 4 lakh customers within 2 years. New services like IPTV (Internet Protocol Television), Wi-Fi, Virtual Private Network (VPN), Games on Demand, Video Conferencing etc. come bundled with Broadband connection. It also offers to customers dedicated leased circuits services, to help them carry out their business better. MTNL also offers Intelligent Network (IN) services like Virtual Calling Card (VCC), televoting etc. It is also keeping itself ready to roll out (Wi-Max), 3G, VoIP services to ensure that it is present in every segment and keeping up with technological developments.

Broadly MTNL's services can be segmented into Landline, Mobile, Leased Circuits, Internet Services and Intelligent Network Services. MTNL has also ventured into Digital Certifications Business under the brand name MTNL Trust Line and has set up its own certification Authority, which has received a license.

Operations of MTNL

MTNL can operate only in Mumbai and Delhi within India as per the present licensing conditions and hence for growth, it has no option but to look to other countries. MTNL has entered into few international ventures. However, this model is yet to be proven and revenue from these form only a small part of the total revenue.

MTNL has entered into following international ventures to increase its growth prospects:

(a) United Telecom Limited (UTL)

MTNL has formed a Joint Venture company in the name of United Telecom Ltd. (UTL) with Telecom Consultants India Limited (TCIL), Videsh Sanchar Nigam Limited (VSNL) and NVPL (Nepal Ventures Pvt. Ltd., a Nepalese Company). The Company is operational since 10th October 2001 for providing WLL based basic services in Nepal.

(b) Mahanagar Telephone (Mauritius) Limited (MTML)

MTNL has set up its 100% subsidiary Mauritius arm under the name Mahanagar Telephone (Mauritius) Limited (MTML), for rollout of the telecom network in Mauritius as 2nd Operator for providing basic, mobile and international long distance services.

(c) Millenium Telecom Limited (MTL)

MTNL has also incorporated on 17th Feb. 2000; Millennium Telecom limited which is a wholly owned subsidiary of MTNL. This was formed to do practically any type of telecom business with a focus on value added services. While its intention were to be a universal telecom solution provider to meet the needs of the customer for both telecom and its applications, on a one stop basis, presently it is primarily focusing on laying of a submarine cable from India for international long distance operations.

MTNL PERFORMANCE

Technology has taken telecommunication to such an extent that wireless communication has dominated over wire line, which resulted in reduction of landline connections. It is not only MTNL that is losing its landline customers but it has been an universal trend including India as the *Graph 1*.

Graph 1: Fixed Line (Landline+WLL(F) 4 Percentage - All India Vs MTNL 2001-2006

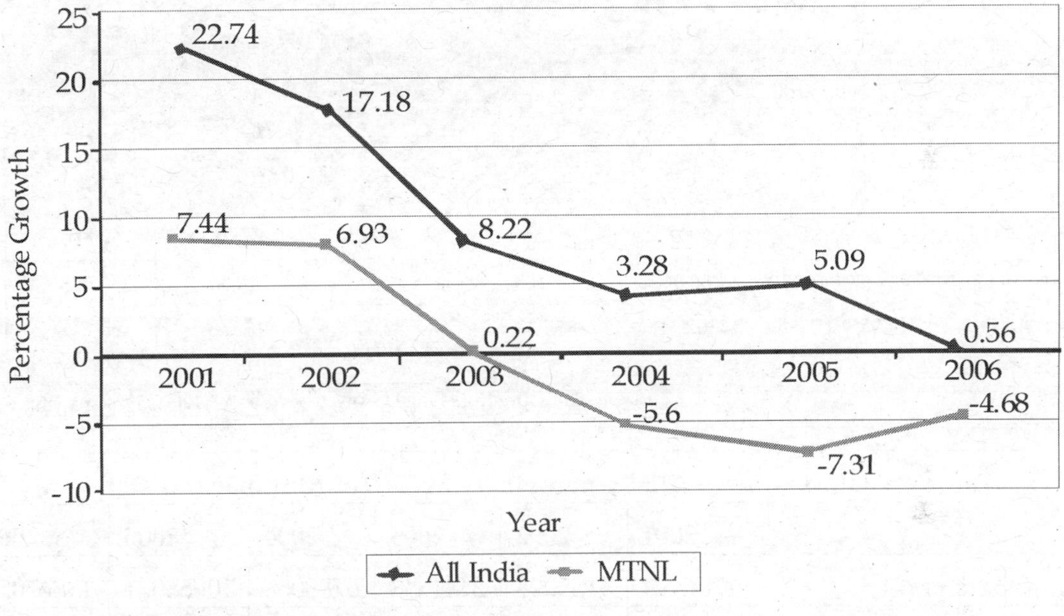

Source: *TRAI Annual Reports 2001-2006*

The reduction is because of the disruptive mobile technology. While customers who could afford more than one line, availed of landline as well as mobile services, the low income category customer who could afford only one telephone preferred to choose a mobile. Moreover, mobile telephone is more hassle free and convenient to use.

---

[4] *WLL (F), Wireless Local Loop (Fixed) is a wireless fixed landline.*

On the mobile segment, MTNL especially in the year 2005, had taken special efforts to expand its GSM capacity and market it aggressively. Moreover, MTNL have not fared badly in terms of percentage growth, as it is in tune with industry trend but there is room to improve its subscribers base, which accounts for just more than 17% of the total mobile subscribers in Mumbai and Delhi , the below(read GSM).[5] ***(Graph2 and Table 2)***

Graph 2 : GSM Percentage Growth : ALL Operators Vs MTNL in Mumbai & Delhi 2002-2006

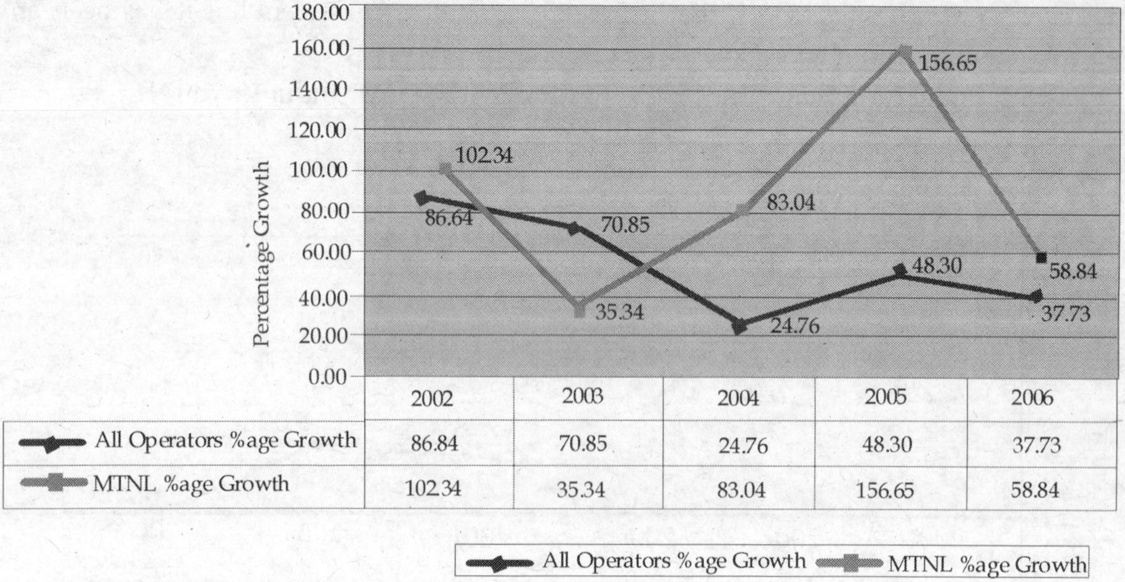

Table 2 : GSM Growth All Operators[6] Vs MTNL of Mumbai and Delhi only

	2001	2002	2003	2004	2005	2006
All Operators	1706494	3185008	5441638	6789068	10068021	13867051
Percentage Growth		86.64	70.85	24.76	48.30	37.73
MTNL	118656	240088	324933	594742	1526422	2424533
Percentage Growth		102.34	35.34	83.04	156.65	58.84

Source : *www.coai.com*

[5] *(read GSM) subscribers since in India GSM technology is more dominant having more than 73% of the mobile market share.*

[6] *MTNL, Bharti, Hutch & BPL.*

Table 3 shows how MTNL has been increasing its efficiency over the years. The number of faults is steadily decreasing and so on. The data at **Table 4** is for MTNL Mumbai, one of its operating units but we can safely assume that the combined average would be more or less the same.

Table 3: OPERATIONAL PARAMETERS (MTNL Mumbai Only)

	2002	2003	2004	2005	2006
No. of Faults per 100 Stations (Telephones)	11.84	9.79	8.79	9.04	10.75
Average duration of Telephone faults in hrs.		33.07	31.64	26.83	29.13
No. of Metered Call units per DEL per year (Telephones)	9668	7984	8204	8158	7878

Source : *MTNL Annual Administrative Report 2005-2006*

Advent of new technologies like Voice over Internet Protocol (VOIP), 3rd Generation technology(3G), Internet Protocol Television (IPTV), Wireless Fidelity (Wi-Fi), Worldwide Interoperability for Microwave Access (Wi-Max) etc. are likely to put more pressure as these technology will provide better and more economic means of communication due to which landline revenues and base will have further threat, putting MTNL's profits under pressure.

In the year 2007 because of private operator's focus on large and profitable customers, there is a serious threat on MTNL for pressure on profits and revenue. To enable comparison of key data of MTNL which includes Direct Exchange Line (DEL) growth including mobile ***(Graph 3)***, revenue per DEL ***(Graph 4)***, DEL per employee ***(Graph 5)***, capital investment, profit before tax, fixed assets, total revenue etc. for the pre competition period and competition period have been separately presented in graphical format and table format in the Annexure.

Graph 3 : Total Number of DEL's (FL+FWT+GSM+WLL) of MTNL in Million 1987-2006

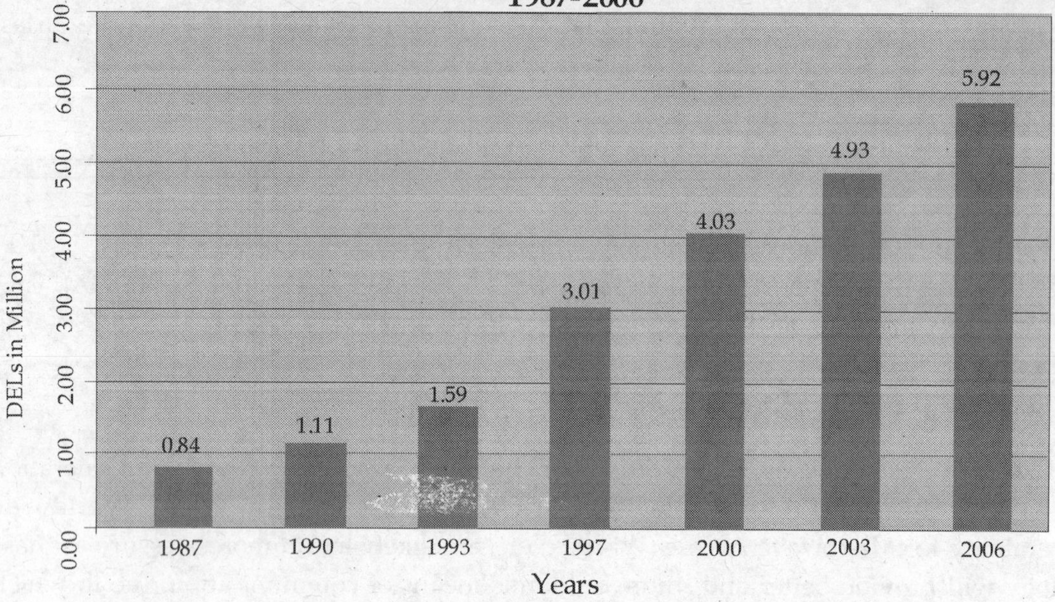

Source: MTNL Annual Reports, 1987-2006.

Graph 4 : Revenue in Rs. Per DEL per year 1998-2006

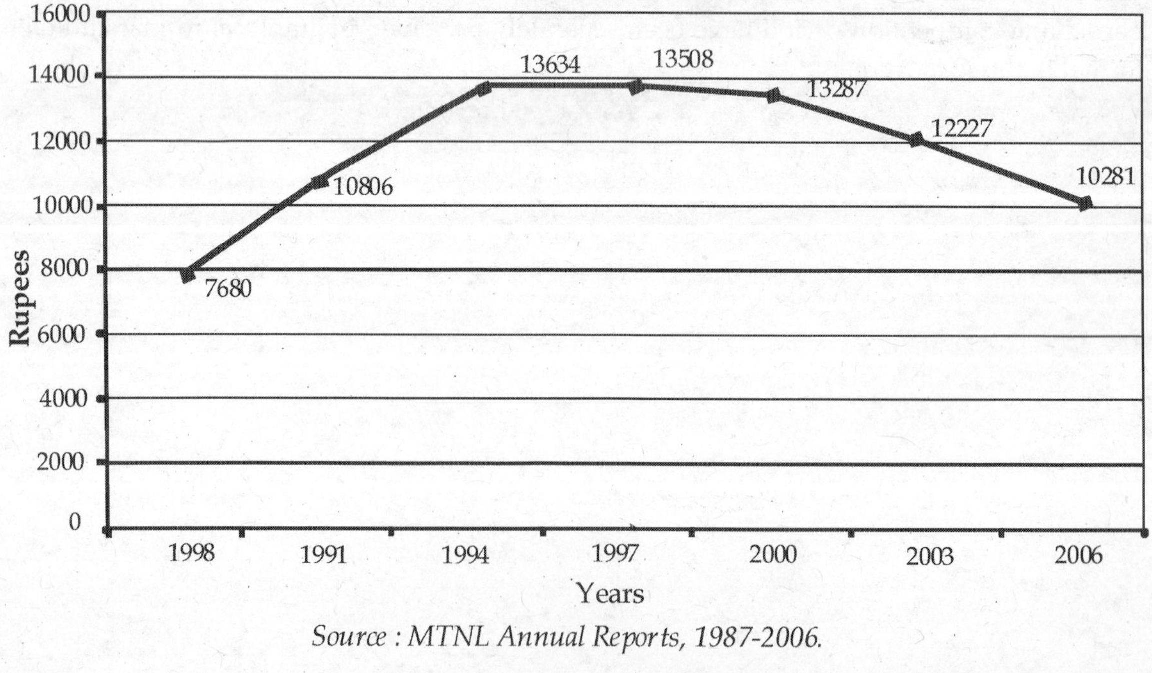

Source : MTNL Annual Reports, 1987-2006.

Graph 5 : MTNLs Number of Telephones per Employee 1998-2006

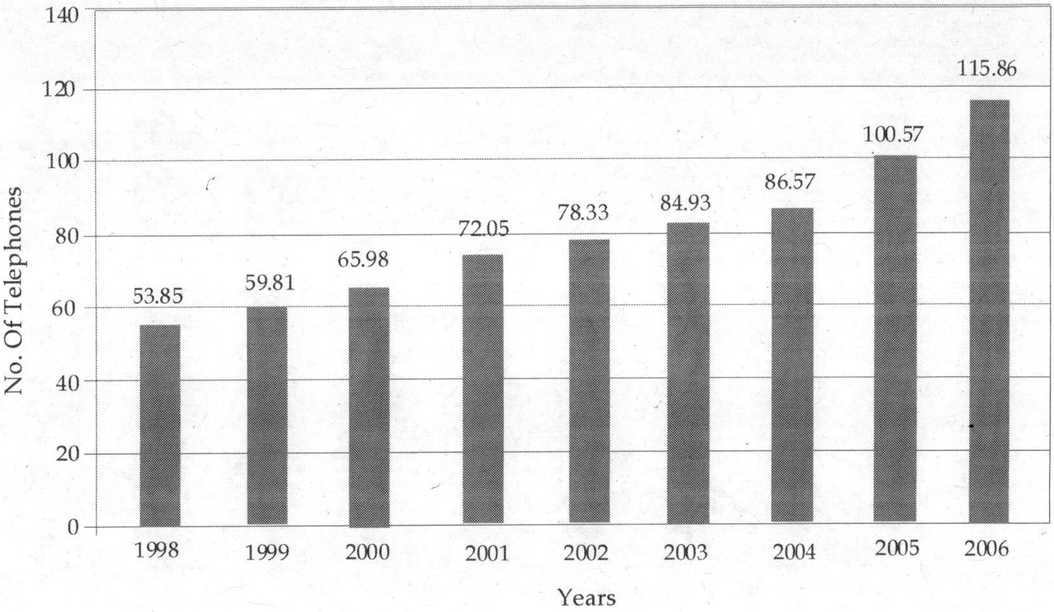

Source: *MTNL Annual Reports, 1998-2006.*

Financial Status

Prior to its formation MTNL was a part of Department of Government of India, Ministry of Communication. On 1st April, 1986 MTNL was incorporated as a public sector enterprise and the assets were transferred to the newly found company.

At present the company has an authorized capital of Rs.800 crore and a equity of Rs.630 crore out of which 56.25% equity is owned by Govt. of India. The company is a debt free company and is able to meet its entire requirement from its own resources. Besides MTNL being listed in Bombay Stock Exchange (BSE) and National Stock Exchange (NSE), MTNL has also listed itself in New York Stock Exchange (NYSE) in the year 2001. Because of which it had to ensure various additional compliance as per listing agreement, which include The Sarbanes-Oxley Act 2002 (SOX) compliance, as per United States federal law..

Since MTNL formation in 1986 and till the influx of competition in 1995-96, MTNL has been consistently growing, earning increasing revenues and increasing profits. Further, MTNL has also been making huge investments to enhance its capacity and technical infrastructure resulting in increasing fixed assets and network growth. After 1998, with the influx of competition, there has been pressure on revenue and profits. However, MTNL continued to make profits during this period as displayed in ***Graph 6.***

Graph 6 : MTNLs Total Revenue Vs Profit

1987 - 2006

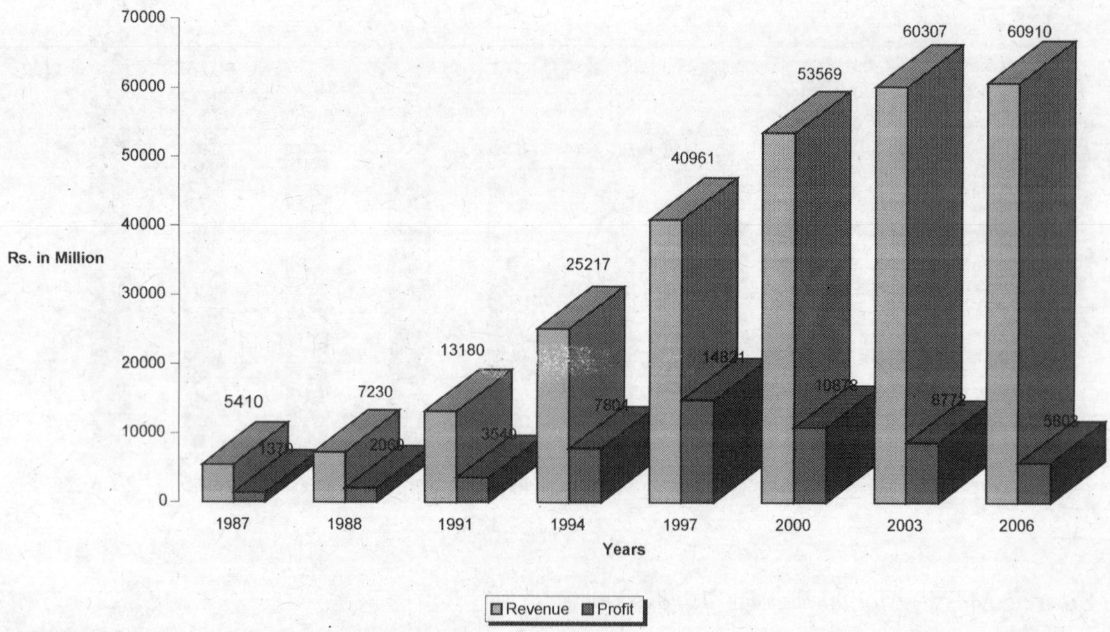

Source: *MTNL Annual Reports, 1987 -2006.*

The company continues to enjoy profits and a comparison of key parameters of Profit & Loss A/c and Balance sheets for past years are tabulated in Table 5 & 6 (in Annexure). The Profit & loss comparisons bring out areas of concern as in some period a good percentage of revenue is out of other sources than its core operations. (Refer Table 6 in Annexure)

Company Assets

The company has lots of property situated strategically in prime locations across the city. MTNL owns over 400 acres of land in Mumbai and Delhi[7]. Considering that these properties are valued at their original prices which in most cases were subsidized, revaluation would enhance the asset base by large amount. With the development in technologies, new technology telephone exchanges require less space and hence freed spaces can be suitably utilized for other purposes. However, to provide better reach to its customers, MTNL has taken small office spaces on rent at number of places and is paying a

[7] *Economic Times, Jan 19, 2007*

large amount towards rent (over Rs.600 million in 2005-06). With the availability of enough space in its own building there is pressure to surrender spaces and strike a balance between customer convenience and rent pay outs.

Some Competitors of MTNL[8] :

Bharti Airtel

Bharti Airtel, formerly known as **Bharti Tele-Ventures Limited** (BTVL) is among India's largest mobile phone and Fixed Network operators. With more than 28.6 million subscriptions as of September 2006, the company is one of the world's fastest growing telecom companies. It offers its mobile services under the **Airtel** brand and is headed by Sunil Mittal, one of India's richest men. As its strategy is to service Pan-India, the company is the only operator to provide mobile services in all the 23 circles in India. The company also provides telephone services and Internet access over DSL in 14 circles. The company complements its mobile, broadband and telephone services with national and international long distance services. The company also has a submarine cable landing station at Chennai, which connects the submarine cable connecting Chennai and Singapore.

Reliance Communications

Reliance Communications (formerly *Reliance Infocomm*), along with Reliance Telecom and Flag Telecom, is part of Reliance Communications Ventures (RCoVL). It is the flagship company of the Reliance-Anil Dhirubhai Ambani Group, comprising of power (Reliance Energy), financial services (Reliance Capital) and telecom initiatives of the Reliance ADAG Group. Reliance Infocomm is currently managed by Anil Dhirubhai Ambani.

Reliance started its telecommunication operation with CDMA technology and now is trying to foray aggressively into the GSM domain. Initially, Reliance started its operation by using Closed User Group (CUG) strategy so that their network grows all over India at a fast rate, leveraging on the advantage of reduced rate. As on September 30 2006, Reliance total subscribers base stands at 26 million.

Bharat Sanchar Nigam Limited (BSNL)

Bharat Sanchar Nigam Limited (known as **BSNL**) is a Public Sector Communications company, wholly owned by the Government of India and is having a status of **Mini Ratna** - a status assigned to reputed Public Sector companies in India.

---

[8] *Total Subscribers break up of MTNL & its competitors in Mumbai & Delhi as on September 30, 2006 Table 7 and 8 in annexure.*

BSNL is India's oldest and largest Communication Service Provider (CSP). As on September 30,2006, BSNL is having a customer base of 58 million (Fixed & Mobile). It has footprints throughout India except for the metropolitan cities of Mumbai and New Delhi which are being managed by MTNL. MTNL does not directly compete with BSNL, however to provide Pan-India services, MTNL needs constant co-ordination with BSNL as the demand arises.

Decision-Making and Control Process

MTNL, being a PSU governed by Government rules and regulations and by virtue of its long experience in Telecom sector, has got well laid policies and procedures to conduct business. Various forms, processes, work-flows, reports, control structures are well defined and documented. MTNL also observes transparency in its tariff structure and in turn displays all its tariffs on its websites and other accessible centers, along with advertising them through its marketing wing. Due to this transparency, customers have developed faith and confidence in MTNL's tariff and billing practices.

However, if any changes are required in the tariff structure due to competition or other pressure, the proposals have to go through a series of examinations and approvals. Apart from the concerned unit, the case has to be screened by finance wing and commercial wing for tariff changes. There is a tariff committee consisting of senior officers from operation, finance, commercial and marketing units. These proposals after clearance from tariff committee and local Executive Director are once again examined by Executive Committee headed by CMD which is an apex body at Corporate Office. After which only, the tariff changes can be finalized, implemented and marketed.

There are strict budgetary controls over expenditures that can be made under different expenditure heads and for most of the expenditure, preparation of estimates, its approval, financial concurrence, tendering procedure etc. is required.

Customer Preferences and Requirements

During a survey recently conducted by MTNL for its internal use, it was brought out that those high end customers whose profitability is better, expected nationwide services, 24*7 service availability, service level agreements, single point of contact and faster provisioning of services apart from competitive tariff structures. While MTNL has been able to provide most of the above facility for corporate customers, a lot needs to be done for other customers. To provide nationwide i.e. Pan-India services, MTNL has to get into an agreement with BSNL. MTNL & BSNL having exclusive geographical areas jointly can provide services all over India. BSNL has got well laid copper, optical fiber and wireless network all over in India.

Primary Concerns

Average total expense of MTNL on employee remuneration and benefits is high being around 30% of its total-revenue, as against 5-6% for the competitors. Further MTNL has higher manpower strength going by bench-mark standards; almost 50,000 employees in just the two cities (Mumbai & Delhi). Hence this becomes an area where competitors get a competitive advantage over MTNL. MTNL has through its various schemes been able to reduce its strength marginally but that too at very lucrative terms involving high cost. Other operational costs of MTNL are on the higher side as well because of the laid down stringent standards as per international practices for various activities and processes.

Employees of MTNL enjoy high job security because of detailed process involved in removal/retrenchment and also because of involvement of unions in various employee related issues. In such an environment, with fixed pay packets, it becomes a big challenge to get high performance. Employees tend to get complacent and take their job for granted. Further, various unions and associations restrict the freedom to take disciplinary actions in case of erring/non performing employees. Though ideally, the competitive environment requires courteous behaviour even in strenuous circumstances, considering the job cushion the employees enjoy, it is taking time to change the attitude of such large number of employees towards customer.

At times even the management cadre may shy away from taking initiatives and innovative steps because of various government controls which are supported by audits and vigilance procedures. In case a venture fails, the officer may have to face embarrassing questions from superiors, audit parties and vigilance groups. Promotions in the organization are primarily seniority based which also hampers aggressiveness of the officers. Further at the top level, the officers may have short tenure which may dither them from taking strong actions and decisions.

Being a public sector undertaking, procurement policy is guided by material procurement policy designed as per the guidelines provided by the government and MTNL has to use tendering process for all procurements with purchases at lowest cost of fee. High value tenders may get involved into litigations normally initiated by the Vendor who lost the tender, thereby delaying the procurement and project completions.

In spite of all these, MTNL has got a very experienced and technically competent pool of manpower which is one of its main strengths. Various training and redeployment initiations are being taken by MTNL to enhance the efficiency and effectiveness of its employees.

Tariff Changes and its Impact

In spite of inflation and rising prices of different goods or services year over year, telecom sector has been showing a reverse trend mainly due to pressure of competition. As against the price/charges of Rs. 1.20 per 3 minute call charges in the year 1998, currently for high end customers, the charges has come down to 70 Paisa per 3 minute call in landline segment and 30 Paisa per minute in mobile segment, This has taken place with repeated reduction in prices, in various phases, specially for high revenue customers. These reductions have brought MTNL's profit margins and revenue under pressure & requiring MTNL to continuously take steps to maintain its profits.

However, as against other service providers who have been offering prices after negotiations on case to case basis, MTNL has been following standard prices and discounts, regularly declared for various volume slabs. In view of the large customer base, any such price reduction applicable to all its customers makes an immediate impact on revenue and greater impact on profits as most of the costs are fixed cost.

Basis of Telecom Competition – Pricing

In the beginning of competition, considering that MTNL was a typical government organization working under monopoly environment, private service operators had felt that they would be able to deliver much better services and hence would command a premium in prices. However, due to strong infrastructural base, technical competence, established processes and customer's faith in government operations, they were proved wrong. Within few years, private operators realized that to gain market share, they have to compete on prices i.e. prices proved to be the main differentiator while choosing a telecom service provider. While the price war had been in existence for quite some time, the year 2006 has been the year where private operators reduced their prices to create a substantial gap from the incumbent service providers prices (*read MTNL & Bharat Sanchar Nigam Limited (BSNL)*). All private operators adjusted their prices to fill the gap by lowering their prices.

At this juncture, MTNL had to take a major decision as whether to retain the original pricing and command a safe profit margin per existing client or change/lower the pricing strategy to avoid churning of customers. Due to the gap between prices offered by private players and that by MTNL, MTNL gradually started losing its customer base. In case of a price reduction, as the customer base of MTNL, especially for landline segment is very large, even a small price reduction will result in large reduction in revenue and a larger reduction in profits. This is so as a large proportion of expenditure is towards fixed cost and variable costs are minimal. However, if MTNL does not succumb to the pressure and does not reduce its prices promptly, it runs the risk of losing its customer base permanently resulting in serious implications for its future growth.

Further to aggravate the situation, new service operators have the option to choose customers and concentrate their marketing efforts to focus on the customers who would be providing higher profit margins or at least would provide huge revenue. This is also a serious concern for MTNL which runs the risk of losing its profitable customer base and could remain stranded with marginal customers seriously hampering its profitability.

Now that competition is here and customers have options to choose from, the bargaining power of customers has risen. As a consequence, customers have started taking advantage of the competitive environment insisting for very low rates, with a threat to shift to other operators if not agreed to.

Realizing the importance of commercially important customers, MTNL had already set up an independent unit under the charge of General Manager (GM) - Business Development (BD) to provide customized and improved services to such customers. It is the responsibility of this unit to ensure retention of its existing profitable customers and also to find ways and means to ensure that not only existing customers avail of any additional services from MTNL but also new customers in this segment are added to the organization. BD unit team, having analyzed the situation thoroughly, had recommended that to achieve these objectives, it is necessary that prices have to be at least on par with competitors if not less than the competitor's prices. As the competitors are losing their patience and are eager to increase their customer base, they were willing to operate at extremely thin margins or in case of large customers even at nil margins for initial periods. Private operators are willing to take higher risks in terms of pricing their services and are willing to offer heavy incentives to facilitate the shift.

Brain Storming

Having gone through the presentation and write up presented by the Business Analysis team, Mr. Gopalan invited comments and suggestions from senior officers present, to handle the challenges put forward by aggressive competitors. He suggested that the team discusses various strategic possibilities and pricing options with an open mind to reach at some common plan of action to be implemented.

Considering that the presentation had covered various internal and external aspects of the organization, competitive forces and strengths and weaknesses, officers present had a lot to say. There were various suggestions and counter suggestions and heated arguments.

As the discussions were getting into an argumentative phase, Mr. Raman, Head Business Development Unit, intervened to bring the meeting to a focus. He said that in present scenario the most serious concern is pricing strategy on which prompt action needs to be taken. Out of his experience in handling the corporate customers, he said out that most of the corporate customers insist on getting some additional advantage, in comparison to what MTNL is offering to others and hence case to case negotiated pricing is the best method at least for large and bulk customers. He added that a large proportion of the cost in maintaining telephone line is fixed cost and the same gets covered in much smaller revenue. Hence some additional benefit can be passed on to the customers who are paying higher revenue per line.

The officers expressed and their concern, not all were in favour of reducing the prices to the extent competitors have done as they still felt that by reminding the customers of

MTNL's long association and transparent practices, the customer will continue to avail of MTNL services. However, Mr. Raman expressed that his unit is expert in this field, has first hand experience in the thinking and decision making process of such customers, and opined that MTNL has already reached a stage where such verbal conviction will not help and reduction in price is inevitable.

During the discussion many suggestions were put forward, however, following opinions were of great relevance:.

- Mr. Diwakar GM (Operations) expressed the concern that if MTNL offer the prices on a case to case basis, there is a possibility of allegation of partiality towards individual customer. Hence the prices should be reduced en-block and offered to all customers.
- Mr. Raman opined that this might reduce the revenue immediately and hence in the present environment it is worthwhile to take a bit of risk and go ahead with case to case negotiated pricing. He argued that even Telecom Regulatory Authority of India (TRAI), has permitted negotiated prices with large and bulk customer which could be subsequently intimated to TRAI at the end of quarter
- Mr. Amar, the Marketing head felt that though MTNL has done a lot of promotion and advertising in the recent past, the marketing efforts have resulted only in enhancing the brand image. MTNL has to ensure that all its products and services are available in sufficient quantity, through all outlets, to meet the demand and any stocks out have to be avoided, as it limits the benefits of advertisements. The demand generated does not get converted to actual sales. He was in favour of Mr. Raman on flexible pricing to large & bulk customers which included franchisees.
- Mr. Ramesh, G.M. (Finance) brought out his concern regarding immediate drop in revenues and profits if any price reduction are introduced without proportionate cost cutting. He emphasized that any reduction should be balanced by cost cutting measures so that the net effect on revenue and profits is very low. After some discussion and information about rates offered by competitors, he agreed that bringing the prices in line with the market rates is immediately necessary. He felt that retention of customers is important at this stage and strict policy on pricing should not lead to churning of customers as retained customer provide a whole stream of revenue from existing services and new services taken in future.
- Mrs. Sheena GM (IT) reminded that MTNL has got a huge data base of all its customers with identity, address and contact details along with their billing patterns, payment habits, payment preferences and usage behaviours. Data base is also available for faulty history, fault details, and fault duration for every customer for past years. This justifies a case for deploying an advances data warehousing, data mining and decision support system (DSS). MTNL can use these data bases and advanced techniques for analyzing

customer patterns and preferences to identify segments and develop customized solutions for these segments.

- Mr. Diwakar, GM (Operations) intervened and informed that many large customers are now demanding pan India services and hence some understanding has to be worked out with BSNL so that services across whole India can be jointly provided.
- The Executive Director, who was heading the meeting, was quietly listening intensely to all the heated discussion. He was also of the opinion that while Mr. Raman's point was very valid and looks like a good business proposition for the company, he was a bit hesitant to take a hasty decision and called for another meeting following month. Before concluding he asked all the officers to come up with supporting information and data to defend their stand.

Dilemma

Mr. Gopalan's mind was busy in working out how should he go about leading this management team to reach to a consensus in a constructive manner with a view to arrive at a strategy and pricing policy which will maintain the competitiveness and attractiveness of MTNL for its existing and future customers? He reflected whatever qualitative reasons and arguments were put forward today were good enough to reach to a consensus. However, if required some more quantitative analysis could be done to weigh various options available to MTNL in a objective manner.

He felt the difference between routine way of thinking of the managers equipped with long experience and expertise in telecom management and an aggressive entrepreneurial way of thinking of the younger generation equipped with tools and techniques of professional management. He reflected on whether various management tools and techniques including BCG Matrix, Porter's Five forces Model, 7-S framework, Game Theory, SWOT Analysis, Perception Mapping, Delta Model and so many others which professional run companies have put into use and benefited from can be successfully and effective used for MTNL as well, or the decisions taken at a blink can help to run the company. He recollected the crucial role played by Business Development group created after restructuring of the company in retaining its high worth customers with high profitability.

At the back of his mind Mr. Gopalan was convinced that the professionals need to manage modern companies in this competitive and uncertain scenario with all the constraints and obstacles. However, it is necessary for MTNL to surge ahead and achieve its missions and goals. "When the going gets tough the tough gets going" should be the appropriate theme for MTNL resurgence. But the priority at hand for Mr. Goapalan is how does he lead the team of well experienced and qualified managers to arrive at a strategic and pricing policy which could lead MTNL to greater heights.

Questions:

1. Comment on the option proposed by Mr. Raman. Is there a better option available?
2. Should MTNL wait for price reduction till it is compensated by cost cutting? What areas would you suggest for implementing cost cutting? In which areas expenditure should be enhanced to get better results?
3. How do you compare the merits and demerits of en-block price reduction vis-à-vis case by case negotiated price reduction?
4. How MTNL can use its database effectively? How the analysis and reports generated can be used for strategic pricing policy formulation?
5. Considering geographical constraint of area of operation in India, what strategy MTNL can follow to expand its operations and achieve growth?
6. What strategic options should Mr. Gopalan follow to achieve a sustainable, structured growth of MTNL so that he will be able to face challenges of competition and enhance growth prospects?
7. What should Mr. Gopalan do to carry the team with him?
8. What similarities do you see with your organizations? How the situations were handled there in similar cases? Could it be handled differently to get better results?

Annexure

TABLE 5 : MTNL OVERALL PERFORMANCES 1998-2006

Financial Year Ending (March)	1997	1998	1999	2000	2001	2002	2003	2004	2005	2006
Total Revenue (Rs. In Million)	40962	47793	52593	53569	58745	63921	60307	66839	60738	60910
Employees (at the end of the year)	64210	63266	62185	61104	60103	59103	58072	55842	53488	51133
Employees Remuneration & Benefits(Rs. in million)	4284	5167	6165	10899	12335	13771	14339	16194	18361	19053
Expenditure/Employee (Rs.)	66719	81671	99134	178369	205227	232994	246910	289991	343278	372619
Total No. of DEL's (FL+FWT+GSM+WLL)	3012324	3406740	3719182	4031624	4330666	4629709	4932225	4834486	5379457	5924428
Revenue in Rs. Per DEL per year	13598	14029	14141	13287	13565	13807	12227	13826	11291	10281
Staff per 100 DELs	2.13	1.86	1.67	1.52	1.39	1.28	1.18	1.16	0.99	0.86
No. of Telephones per Employee	46.91	53.85	59.81	65.98	72.05	78.33	84.93	86.57	100.57	115.86
Land Line (in million)	3.01	3.4	3.72	4.03	4.33	4.63	4.64	4.38	4.06	3.87
Mobile (GSM + WLL (M)) in million							0.29	0.47	1.08	2.05
Broadband (including ADSL)										211935

Data given is approximately accurate Analysis

Source: MTNL Annual Reports 1998-2006

Annexure

Table 6 : Financial Results (Rs. In Million) 1998-2006

Financial Year Ending(March)	1997	1998	1999	2000	2001	2002	2003	2004	2005	2006
Total Revenue (Rs.InMillion)	40962	47793	52593	53569		63921	60307	66839	60738	60910
a) Income from Services	40309	46546	50325	51822		61437	58065	63696	55924	55610
b) Other Income	653	1247	2268	1747		2483	2241	3143	4917	5300
Expenditure (excluding interest & prior period adjustment	25372	30207	32965	39485		45609	47381	49634	48326	53952
Operating profit	14937	16339	17360	12337		15828	10684	14062	7598	1658
Profit before tax (PBT)	14114	16548	18899	13999		18023	12598	16860	12157	6714
Net Profit (PAT)	8620	11301	12972	10878		13007	8772	11505	9390	5803
SOURCES AND USES OF FUNDS										
Authorised Capital	8000	8000	8000	8000		8000	8000	8000	8000	8000
Issued. Subscribed & Paid-up Capital	6000	6300	6300	6300		6300	6300	6300	6300	6300
Reserves & Surplus	29377	45318	56193	64904		83096	88670	96976	103138	106068
REPRESENTED BY										
Fixed Assets (Net Block) (includes Work-in-progress)	45235	49693	53571	56017		61096	64359	6692	70957	65687
Depreciation	31611	37100	42997	49274		64204	71480	73527	77836	82854
Investment						1027	3710	3807	3975	4187
Net Current Assets	66182	67418	47123	46089		53464	26901	38183	40247	42212

*2001 Financial Results – Not Available

***Source:** MTNL Annual Reports 1998-2006*

Annexure

Table 7 : Comparative Growth 2nd Qtr (July – September 2006) Of MTNL & its Competitors

MUMBAI			
	Wireline	WLL (F & LM)	Mobile GSM + CDMA
MTNL	-43,255	998	66,885
Reliance	17,731		116,235
Bharti	13,595		178,018
Tata	7,515	3,785	67,637
Hutch			153,210
BPL			-251,977
DELHI			
	Wireline	WLL (F & LM)	Mobile (GSM + CDMA)
MTNL	-58,541	-736	53,709
Reliance	9,760		79,368
Bharti	59,308		292,678
Tata	-107	-13,713	216,734
Hutch			100,713
Idea			229,541

Table 8 : Subscribers Base as on September 30,2006 of MTNL and Competitors

MUMBAI						
	Wirelline	**WLL-F**	**WLL-LM**	**GSM**	**CDMA**	**Total**
MTNL	2,206,808		26,729	1,198,144		3,432,315
Reliance	58,378				1,941,144	1,999,522
Bharti	37,693			1,515,745		1,603,438
Tata	1,99,242	406,865			573,325	1,179,432
Hutch				2,274,775		2,274,775
BPL				1,045,301		1,045,301
Total	**2,502,121**	**406,865**	**26,729**	**6,084,599**	**2,514,469**	**11,534,783**
DELHI						
	Wirelline	WLL-F	WLL-LM	GSM	CDMA	Total
MTNL	1,543,061		53,623	1,091,477		2,688,161
Reliance	45,521				1,914,575	1,960,096
Bharti	535,049			2,501,510		3,036,559
Tata	14,615	523,078			1,235,733	1,773,426
Hutch				2,055,740		2,055,740
BPL				1,166,091		1,166,091
Total	**2,138,246**	**523,078**	**53,623**	**6,814,818**	**3,150,308**	**12,680,073**

GLOSSARY

3G

3rd Generation, technology for Data, image etc transfer at a much higher speed for mobile telephone users.

ADRs

An American Depositary Receipt (ADR) is how the stock of most foreign companies trades in United States stock markets.

ASDL 2+

Assymetric Digital Subscriber Line , ITU (International Telecommunication Union) standard for transfer of data rates.

BSE

Bombay Stock Exchange, one of the oldest Indian financial exchange for trading company stocks and other securities.

BSNL

Bharat Sancher Nigam Limited. A Indian Government owned company providing telecommunication services all over India except Delhi and Mumbai.

CDMA

Code Division Multiple Access, a technology for wireless communication dominantly used in United states.

DEL

Direct Exchange Lines denotes a single telephone connection of a subscriber.

DOT

Department Of Telecommunication, a Government of India arm to look after the telecommunication sector of India.

EDGE

Enhanced data rate for GSM Evolution, technology for data access with rate faster than GPRS but slower than 3G.

FDI

Foreign Direct Investment, a long term investment by a foreign direct investor in an enterprise resident in an economy other than that in which the foreign direct investor is based.

FWT

Fixed Wireless Telephone.

GPRS

General Packet Radio Service is a mobile data service available to mobile users to browse the internet.

GSM

Global system for mobile communication, a technology for wireless communication predominantly used in Europe.

IPTV

Internet Protocol Television is a technology that provides media communication for Television through Internet Protocol through telephone wires.

ISO 9001-2000

Quality management standards defined by International Organization for Standardization (ISO).

Navratna

Most Valued Government owned companies of India.

NSE

National Stock Exchange, another Indian financial Exchange for trading company stocks and other securities.

NTP 1994

National Telecom Policy 1994, Telecom guidelines for the Indian telecom operators NYSE

New-York Stock Exchange, a United States financial exchange for trading companies stocks and other securities.

PSU

Public Sector Undertaking, Government Owned company (read India).

SOX

The Sarbanes Oxley Act, 2002. A United states Federal Law passed in response to a number of major corporate and accounting scandals.

TRAI

Telecom Regulatory Authority of India.

TRIBAND

Brand name for MTNL's Broadband service.

VOIP

Voice Over Internet Protocol, a technology for voice communication through the Internet Protocol.

VSAT

Very Small Aperture Terminal, a 2-way satellite ground station with a dish antenna that is smaller than 3 meters.

Wi-Fi

Wireless Fidelity, Technology to provide wireless internet connectivity over a small area.

Wi-Max

Worldwide Interoperability for Microwave Access, Technology to provide wireless internet connectivity like Wi-Fi but over a much larger area.

Advertisement (Contd....)

MTNL GSM Service under the brand name **DOLPHIN** taking on the price competition...

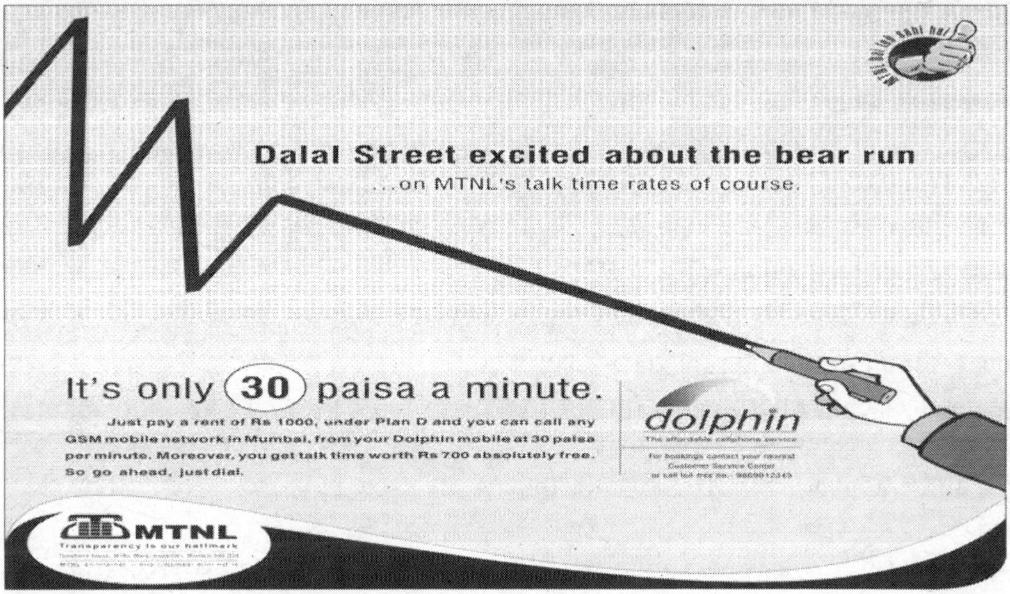

MTNL taking advantage of its vast landline infrastructure which no competitors could match.....

Useful References:

Arthur A. Thompson, Jr., A.J.Strickland III, John E. Gamble and Arun K. Jain (2006), *Crafting and Executing Strategy, The quest for Competitive advantage: Concepts & Cases.* TATA McGraw Hill Publishing Company Limited, New-Delhi.

Ashok V. Desai (2006), *India's Telecommunications Industry: History, Analysis, Diagnosis.* Sage Publication, New-Delhi

Colin M. Clarke-Hill and Keith W. Glaister (1991), *Cases in Strategic Management.* FT Pitman Publishing 128 Long Acre, London, WC2E 9AN.

Cyril Levicki, (1996), *The Strategy Workout, A journey to the heart of your business.* FT Pitman Publishing 128 Long Acre, London, WC2E 9AN.

MTNL Annual Reports 1986-87 to 2005-06

MTNL Annual Administrative Report 2005-2006

MTNL Form 20-F ANNUAL REPORT PURSUANT TO SECTION 13 OR 15(d) OF THE SECURITIES EXCHANGE ACT OF 1934 For the fiscal year ended March 31, 2006 Commission file number 1-15252,SECURITIES AND EXCHANGE COMMISSION , Washington D.C.

Niraj K. Gupta (2000), *The Business of Telecommunication: Networking in the New Millenium.* Tata McGraw-Hill Publishing Company Limited, New-Delhi.

R. Balashankar (1998), *Golden Era of Indian Telecommunications 1947-1997.* Telecommunication Consultants of India Limited.

Upendra Kachru (2005), *Strategic Managements: Concepts and Cases.* Anurag Jain for Excel Books.

Various MTNL Yearly and Anniversary Magazines, Product, Marketing Brouchures.

Useful Web References:

http://www.budde.com.au

http://myiris.com

http://college.hmco.com

http://theory.tifr.res.in

http://www.voicendata.com

http://www.persquareyard.com

www.mumbaimtnl.in

CASE 8

THE DABBAWALLAS OF MUMBAI*

Dr A Rangnekar
Centaur Pharmaceuticals Pvt. Ltd., Mumbai, India

Abstract

The dabbawallas have delivered on a robust model that has adapted well to the changing times over a century of operations. The demand for the delivery of home cooked meals at lunch, their specialization, would only grow in an era of increased health awareness by leveraging dual competitive advantages of reach and economy, which have deterred competition. However, strategic options need to be explored to chart out a growth trajectory as volumes decline due to barriers like inability to replicate the model, suburban migration of offices, increasing meal-time eating out options and the reluctance of next generation to join the profession.

Introduction

It is 8 am in Kalyan, 70 kilometres to the north of Mumbai, and Urmila Pandit is preparing lunch for her daughter, Girija, an undergraduate student at the JJ School of Arts, bang opposite the main CST train terminus in downtown Mumbai. Girija stays at the school hostel pursuing her studies, but 4 hours later would be tucking into fresh home-cooked food prepared lovingly by her mother.

Girija enjoys this privilege thanks partly to Ramesh Kolte, one of Mumbai's 5000 dabbawallas (dabba= tiffin; walla= one who delivers), who pick-up, deliver and return 200,000 dabbas of home cooked meals from the suburbs and the satellite towns tooffices and schools in Mumbai everyday, undeterred by the sweltering heat, torrential downpours or crowds in the local trains.

* The inputs and insights provided by Shri Raghunath Medge, President of the NMTBSCT and Shri Gangaram Talekar, Secretary, into the operations of the dabbawallas of

Mumbai, were invaluable in the conceptualization, evolution and presentation of this case, which is gratefully acknowledged.

As he picks up the tiffin from Urmila and heads for the Kalyan railway station, Ramesh is a vital cog in one of the most ingenious supply chain management systems in the world. The dabbawallas, each an entrepreneur, work in close-knit groups and through a multiple relay system replete with complex codes, ensure door-to-door delivery of tiffins across thousands of Mumbai's offices and schools.

What makes their performance astounding is their operating precision of only 1 error in eight million transactions (**Shamsi, 2003**), which qualifies them for the Six Sigma measure of perfection. Companies with Six Sigma processes make less than 4 mistakes in every million tasks performed for a perfection level of 99.99996 percent (**Daftari and Palande, 2007**). Although the average education level of the dabbawallas is only till the eighth grade of schooling, they provide management lessons to corporates and business schools on leadership and efficiency. Raghunath Medge, the dabbawallas president says "People study business books and then practice. Ours is the reverse. We practiced first and have now become case studies".

This robust, scalable and technology proof model has survived over 115 years and still remains relevant. However changing lifestyles, suburban migration of offices and lack of next generation dabbawallas threaten this model's future, which has always been driven by the Mumbaikar's (Residents of Mumbai and its periphery) yearning for fresh home cooked meals at lunch time and catalysed by Mumbai's world class local rail system.

The management

The operations of the dabbawallas work on very similar lines like a body corporate. What differentiates the dabbawallas from corporates is the nil attrition rate at a time when even booming industries like infotech, BPO and retail, despite dream salary packages, are plagued with 50% churn levels. This is primarily due to the high satisfaction levels among the dabbawallas and the pride they take in their work.

The dabbawallas have an executive committee that works under the stewardship of a president, and includes a vice- president, general secretary and a treasurer. This committee has 9 core committee members reporting to it who look after 800 mukadams (supervisors) and contractors, who actually supervise and co-ordinate the working of 5000 dabbawallas. A flat 3 tiered organizational structure with a span of control of six at the lowest level.

The core committee is elected every 2-3 years by a show of hands. The core committee members are also dabbawallas most of whom are now contractors, having dedicated their youth to the profession. The executive committee basically deals with administrative matters. Every fifteenth of the month, the committee adjudicates on internal disputes and resolves conflicts that largely pertain to infiltration into each other's territories, turf wars and ego clashes but are always settled amicably. In the 115 years of existence of the dabbawallas, no dispute has ever reached the police or the courts nor has there ever been a strike.

The dabbawallas have their own set of penal codes which are enforced on erringdabbawallas in the course of duty. The fines apply to all and they have to abide by the judgement. Absenteeism also entails a steep fine as it directly impacts the business flow and invites censure at the highest levels. The Gandhi cap is their identity and if dabbas are delivered without a cap, it entails a fine of Rs.25 (50 cents).

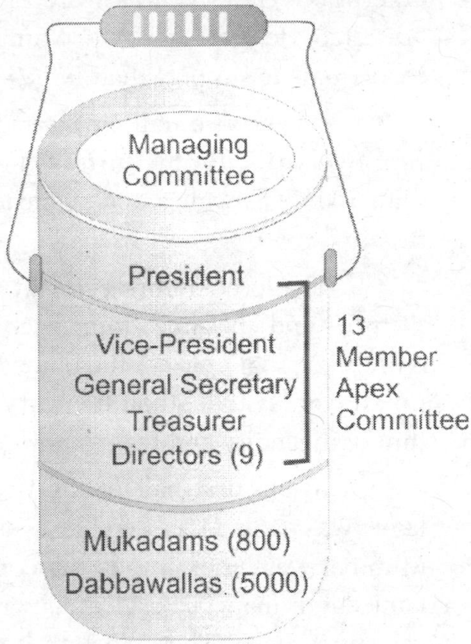

An identity card has been issued to all dabbawallas and is to be compulsorily worn while on duty as the dabbawallas have access to important offices, failure to do so entails a Rs.25. Similarly consuming alcohol while on duty invites a fine of Rs.500. These fines, especially the last one, are more of deterrents to ensure discipline. The mukadam who supervises and co-ordinates their efforts, levies these fines.

However the media attention over the past few years as well as international recognition and the mystique and intrigue of their model have put the core committee members into the limelight. These days the top committee members share insights into their unique system and deliver lectures on their model regularly at business schools and corporates.

The guiding principle of the dabbawallas is "Work is worship". This commitment is evident in their office where rule number 23 confirms that "No customer shall go hungry". These principles have been internalized completely and show in their race against time, braving five million daily passengers in Mumbai's trains and under trying climatic conditions. There have been instances galore of dabbawallas ensuring that the dabba deliveries have been completed, before attending to relatives with serious medical ailments.

The Need and the Seed

The origins of the dabbawallas can be traced to the late nineteenth century during the British Raj, when people from various communities migrated to Mumbai in search of work in the textile mills and trading offices that were mushrooming in Mumbai. Most of these migrants came sans families and stayed with either their relations or with people originally from their villages, and then settled in Mumbai.

Most of the mills worked shifts while offices started early, much before lunch was prepared in homes. At that time there were a lack of transport facilities, no canteens or fast food joints and if working people did not bring their lunch boxes from home, they had to go hungry. Besides, different communities had different tastes and preferences, which could only be satisfied by a home-cooked meal.

Sensing this need gap, Mahadeo Raoji Bacche, a migrant from interior Maharashtra, envisioned and started what was to be the famed dabbawalla service for Mumbaikars in 1890. Bacche wisely chose youths from Pune district, whose families he knew, for his enterprise. These youths were involved in agricultural work and were neither skilled nor educated, to get work in Mumbai. The agricultural income they generated was also inadequate to support their large joint families and they readily accepted Bacche's offer.

The service initially started with only 10 dabbawallas but increased to 20 within the first two years. By the turn of the century, the service was becoming increasingly popular with 100 dabbawallas and cost each client the then princely sum of 50 paise or 8 annas per month.

The local train service in the country was inaugurated in 1853 in Mumbai, by the British, and became immensely popular with Mumbaikars. However, it took the entrepreneurial spirit of the home bred dabbawallas to leverage its efficiency and reach to set up a business that stood the test of time and held its own in an era of technology by sheer dint of ingenuity and team spirit.

In the first half of the twentieth century, the legendary coding system (discussed later) was evolved and coding was then done on the basis of coloured threads. By this time, Mumbai was emerging as the commercial capital of the country with the stock exchange, banks and financial services as well as a plethora of textile mills and trading offices setting up shop there. These factors coupled with the commitment of the dabbawallas were responsible for their acceptance and popularity in the first half of the twentieth century.

By the 1950s, the dabbawallas were delivering around 200,000 dabbas daily. What is significant here is that Mumbai's population then was only 4 million, which means that the dabbawallas delivered lunch to 5% of Mumbai's population. If we consider that in those days very few or no women worked, it implies that the dabbawallas catered to the majority of the working population.

Meanwhile, there were many unorganized dabba suppliers in the city. With the rapid growth in the number of dabbas delivered, there was a need to organize the dabbawallas under a parent body. Thus was born the Nutan Mumbai Tiffin Box Suppliers' Charity Trust (NMTBSCT, but hereafter referred to as the trust) in 1954. This trust continues to be the apex decision making body of the dabbawallas till date and its writ runs large over all the 5000 dabbawallas of Mumbai. The trust concentrated on setting up offices across various important suburbs and strategic train junctions like Grant Road, Dadar, Chembur , Andheri and Mulund.

By this time the coding was being done with the help of coloured cloth rags as the threads could not withstand the teeming crowds in Mumbai's trains and the weather. The trust had spread its tentacles far and wide and dabbas were delivered even from the far flung suburbs of Thane, Kalyan, Dombivali on the central rail track and Borivali and Virar on the western rail track to offices, banks and mills in central and south Mumbai with consummate efficiency. This wide coverage coupled with customer reach emerged as a key sustainable advantage, which has endured till date and deterred corporate competition.

The 1960s and 1970s saw the dabbawallas popularity at its peak and consolidation of customers, especially the mill workers and government and bank employees. However, the population of Mumbai by 1970 had touched 7 million and although the dabbawallas were maintaining 200,000 deliveries a day, their share of Mumbai's population had reduced to 3%. By this time the coding had changed from coloured cloth to oil paint marks on the covering lid of the dabbas, a more permanent way of braving the surging crowds in Mumbai's trains.

The mid 1970s saw another strategic shift that has proved to be a key sustainable advantage and one that has enhanced the commitment levels of the dabbawallas. Mr. Datta Samant led the railway strike of 1975, which lasted for nearly a month and caused huge losses to the dabbawallas as they could not effect deliveries during this period. These losses were further compounded by the textile mill strikes of the late 1970s.

Till 1980 the association consisted of small affiliated groups with a worker-owner relationship as every contractor employed 20-25 workers under him. These events set the dabbawallas association trust into a huddle thinking of what may happen if the dabbawallas themselves went on strike and the customers had to go hungry. This was the reason every worker was made a shareholder which ensured that they would put in more effort and importantly, there would be no formation of a union. This practice continues till date as each group within the dabbawallas equally shares the monthly spoils.

During this time, signs of the labour unrest in the textile industry were evident, an ominous sign, as the bulk of the textile labour force were the major clientele for the dabbawallas. As the 1980s approached, textile mills started shutting down and there were layoffs and lockouts, which affected the income of the mill workers and in turndented daily volumes for the dabbawallas to only 150,000 dabbas. Shaken, and stirred into action, the dabbawallas focused on schools and this started paying dividends and volumes rose.

The 1980s had witnessed a mushrooming of eating out options in the form of food gaadis (carts), stalls, fast food joints and local caterers who offered a choice of cuisines catering to all communities across India as well as Chinese and Continental options, especially in south Mumbai, where majority of the dabbawallas clients were located. But people who felt that outside food was unhygienic and who wanted to have a specific diet started using their service.

Graph 1 : The dabbawallas- waning influence

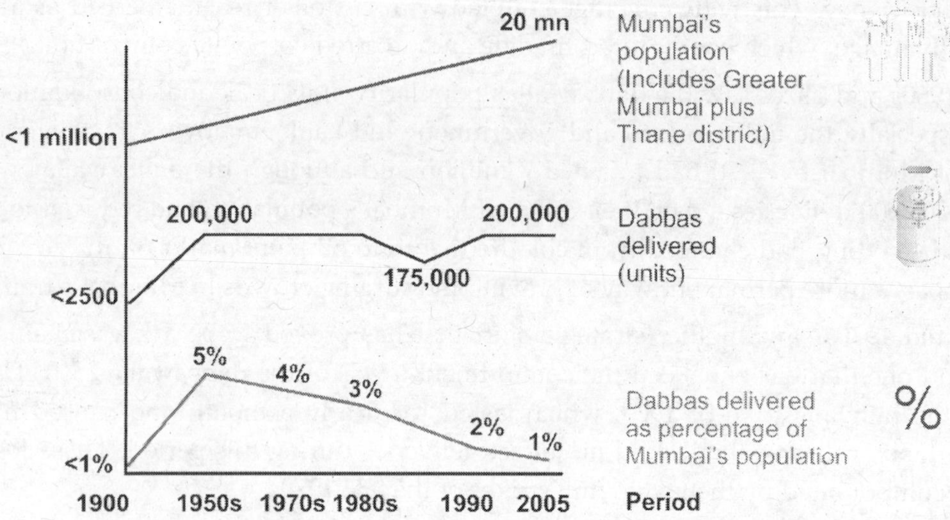

(Map not to scale.Figures are indicative and sourced from the dubbawallas. Demographic figures of Mumbai culled from the internet)

The 1990s saw the IT and internet revolution engulf India and the advent of ubiquitous gizmos like the PC, laptop and the mobile phone. The dabbawallas response to this technological convergence was typical, they changed their coding from oil paint dots and bars to alpha-numerics (see page 124).

Driven by these dynamics, the turn of the millennium saw the dabbawallas regain volumes of 175,000 - 200,000 lunches a day, which had dipped. But by this time the

population of Mumbai and neighbouring Thane district had burgeoned to 20 million including a significant increase in the working population, especially the women. This meant that the dabbawallas accounted for barely 1% of Mumbai's population.

By now the mills had closed down, offices and banks had also started moving out from south Mumbai to central, suburban and Navi Mumbai due to a mix of reasons ranging from better customer coverage to low real estate prices in the suburbs to better infrastructure. The concentration of people in the suburbs vis-à-vis the city was now 70:30. This actually presented an opportunity for the dabbawallas but the emergence of multi-cuisine fast food options as well as in-house cafes, lunch coupons and above all an increased tendency to eat out, slightly queered the pitch for the dabbawallas.

The dabbawallas have delivered the goods or rather the foods for more than a century, and the average middle class Mumbaikar still yearns for his dabba of home cooked "chapaati-bhaaji" at work for lunch. How do the dabbawallas manage to, as the popular commercial goes, "Just do it" day after day and with the same passion and precision of their forefathers.

Meal time management lessons - how do they do it

The dabbawallas system is ranked at par with world performance leaders like GE andMotorola in terms of efficiency and quality of service. Says renowned management guru CK Prahalad, "Six sigma essentially means you can talk no errors. One-hundred and seventy-five thousand boxes are transported every day, it has to go to the right person, it has to start from a point of origination, go through trans-shipment in the infrastructure which is the public infrastructure in the trains of Mumbai in all seasons including the monsoon and it has to arrive on time in the right place in the right box. What makes it unique is its low capital intensity and its price performance relationship."

Graph 2 : Customer Profile of the Dabbawallas*

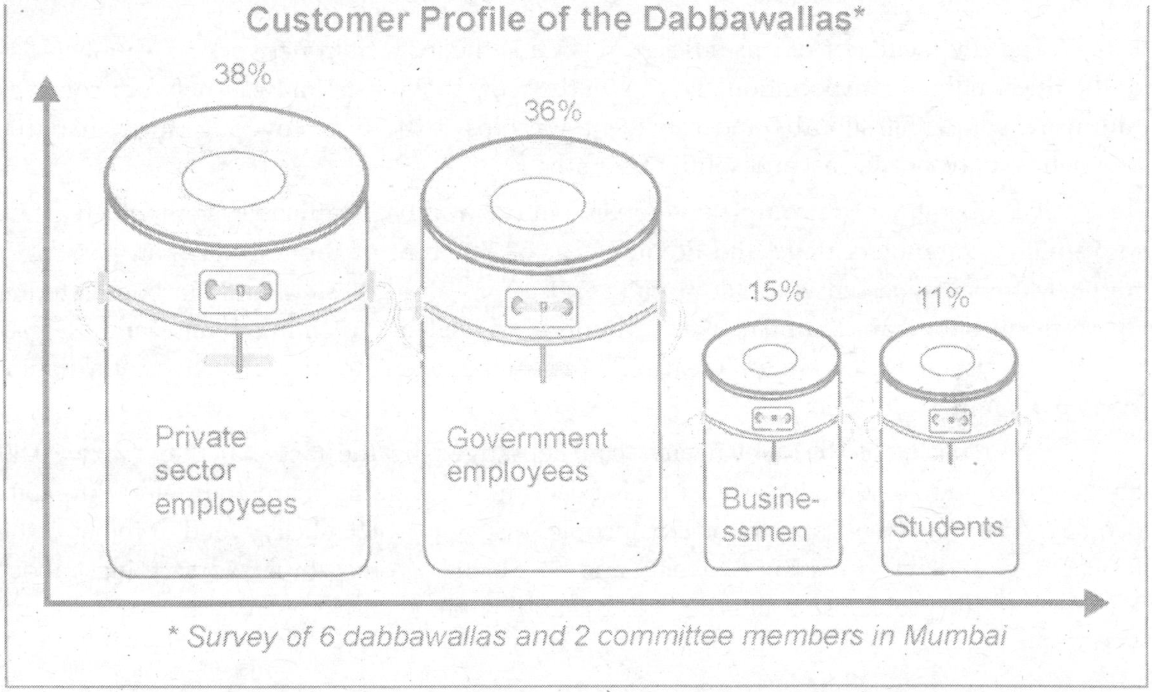

To deliver these kind of efficiencies amid so many constraints, and in a city where many observe fasts and religious dietary rules, an errant delivery could offend religious sensibilities and turn out to be a major embarrassment for the dabbawallas.

The operations are complex because if even one thing goes out of place, it can lead to chaos. The dabbawallas are most feared by the ladies who prepare the lunch tiffins at home, as they are extremely punctual and if there is any delay in keeping the dabbas ready at the appointed time, the dabbawallas refuse to wait and the ladies run the risk of keeping their dear ones hungry and sometimes angry.

The dabbawallas are privileged that they are allowed to deposit the dabbas with the security at most of the high rise buildings in downtown Mumbai, which saves precious time.

On being asked about whether a computer can ease the load and bring in more precision, Gangaram Talekar, the secretary of the trust emphatically states "No, we never use computers or any other technology, in fact most of us are uneducated. Our computer is our head and our Gandhi Cap is the computer cover to protect it from the sun or rain".

However, Talekar admits " We make a rare error once a month, which mostly is due to a hungry beggar stealing a dabba at one of the stations. The dabbawallas then keep a lookout for it in the market and on spotting it buy it back and return it to the rightful owner. The robustness of the system and the commitment levels of the dabbawallas ensure that they never misplace anything due to any confusion on their part. The uneducated have an unerring ability to memorize and retain more, as opposed to the educated who are used to writing down everything.

Operations

The key facilitator of this efficient service is the local train network in Mumbai, one of the finest public transportation systems in the world. The local railway network connects Mumbai's sprawling suburbs and satellite townships to the city covering more than 100 kilometres to the north, east and south of Mumbai.

The operations are completely dependent on Mumbai's railway system which caters to 5 million commuters daily and accounts for 50 per cent of India's daily rail passenger traffic. Mumbai is blessed with 3 local rail services - Central, Western and Harbour catering to Mumbai, suburban Mumbai, Navi Mumbai as well as adjoining Thane and Raigad districts, an urban agglomeration of over 20 million people. A local train arrives at a station every 3-4 minutes.

The tenacity of the dabbawallas can be gauged by the fact that they carry 30-40 dabbas weighing 70-80 kilograms on their head and manage to board trains ferrying 4500 people against an actual capacity of 1250 people. Inspite of such a heavy load, it remains the fastest means of crisscrossing the city and is devoid of the three worst things about Mumbai's traffic problems- pollution, potholes and parking spaces.

Graph 3 : Dabba traffic across Mumbai's reil network

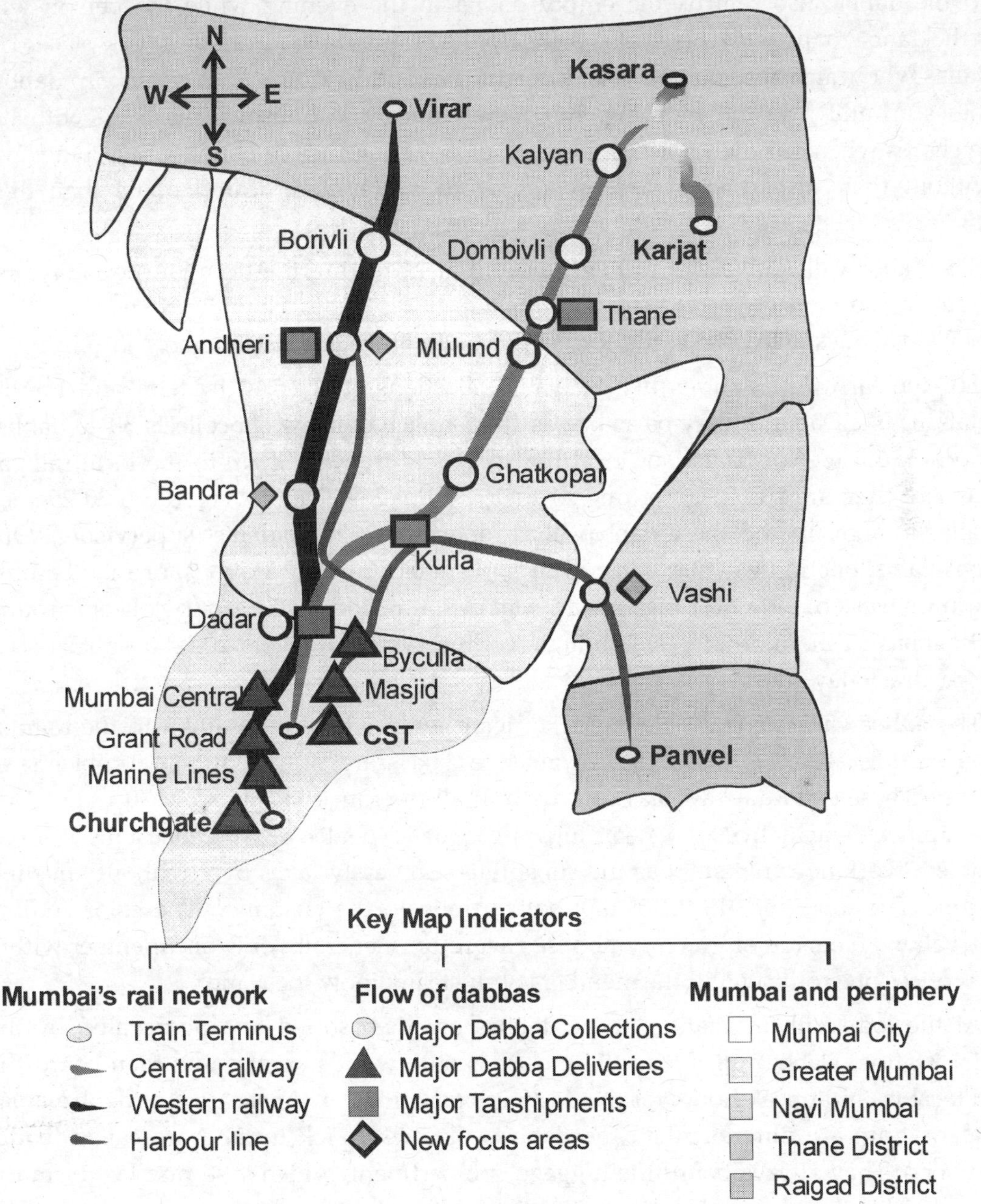

The dabbawallas operate through a relay system where 4-6 dabbawallas are directly involved in the collection, trans-shipment, delivery and return of the dabba. The person who picks up the dabba also returns the empty dabba in the evening while the person who delivers the dabba to the work place also picks up the empty dabba from the work place. The dabbawallas who trans-ship may also be different, pre and post lunch. "We pick up dabbas from homes around 9 in the morning. But many times, the housewife is busy with her morning chores when our man reaches there. So after giving them a couple of warnings, we leave without their tiffins. So in a sense the women are more scared of us than their husbands" says Medge.

The dabbawallas involved in the trans-shipment during the train journey may also be different in the morning and afternoon. Inspite of the dabba changing hands so many times, they are always delivered to the correct person in office and back home.

For the far away stations like Kalyan, collections start early by 8am and for the nearer stations like Dadar, it may be as late as 10 am. Each dabbawalla collects 30-40 dabbas in the morning on foot or bicycle or local transport and delivers them to the local railway station, where they are sorted according to their destination station. There are 20-25 such dabbawallas in a group and these dabbawallas report to 3-4 mukadams (supervisors). One group looks after one railway station or even two smaller railway stations, or may be only the eastern or western side of a big railway stations, junction. Each group collects around 750-1000 dabbas in the morning. This unique coding system delivers 200,000 dabbas with unerring accuracy day after day.

The dabbawallas operate like a cricket team with, where in addition to the regular players there are atleast 2 extra dabbawallas to take care of operational problems or emergencies. These extra dabbawallas can perform all the functions from pick-up to sorting to trans-shipment and delivery. As earnings are equally pooled, if someone falls ill or is incapacitated, work does not stop, as the substitute seamlessly takes over without affecting the network. The food and the tiffin box both belong to the customer. The color coding, generally yellow, blue, red or green symbolizes a 'group'. Generally only one member within a group services one route but all the members of the team know the route.

At the local railway station, these dabbas are then sorted and aggregated by the destination station. Dabbawallas load these dabbas onto wooden crates and then board the crowded local trains at peak hours for the destination stations. In most cases the dabbawallas boarding the train are different than the dabbawallas who pick up and are called 'badli' (change overs). They always board the luggage compartment, which is second last from the engine and where they have places reserved by dabbawallas from the earlier stations. The passengers in the jam - packed compartments are always co-operative towards the dabbawallas, who have no official arrangements with the railways.

The average collection of dabbas at each railway station on the Central, Western and Harbour railway lines prior to Dadar railway junction, is around 1500-2000 dabbas, while the major suburban stations have maximum collections of 6000 plus dabbas at Borivli, Andheri and Thane stations.

Once the dabbas are loaded they are trans-shipped at important junctions so as to reach their destinations. As people crisscross across Mumbai changing 2-3 trains to reach their destination, so do their dabbas. Andheri, Dadar, Bandra and Kurla are major trans-shipment junctions and the dabbas are again resorted at these junctions. Dadar junction connects western and central railway, while Kurla connects Central and Harbour railways. The dabbas reach Central railway stations from the Western railway via the Harbour line at Mahim junction.

From these junctions, the dabbas are transported to their final destination stations. The maximum dabbas are delivered at the main termini like Churchgate (Western railway) and CST (Central and Harbour lines). Once the train reaches these termini, the dabbas are downloaded and brought outside the station, where there are special areas earmarked, by the railways and the municipality, for the dabbawallas to sort during their peak period, just before lunch time.

"We made it clear to the people representing Prince Charles that we could not delay our operations to accommodate his schedule and that he had to meet us at a time, convenient to us, if he wanted to actually observe us in action. We met him at 11am at Churchgate station and gave him exactly 6 minutes. In our line customer is king and when it is a matter of delivering dabbas for lunch, our work supersedes all other engagements be it a Raja or even a Maharaja" says Medge in his matter of fact style outlining the efficiency, commitment and punctuality of the dabbawallas.

Sorting is done at the destination station like Churchgate for areas like Flora Fountain, High Court, Nariman Point, etc and then for buildings within that area as in Air India building or Express Towers within Nariman Point. In such buildings or areas, where more than a hundred dabbas are to be delivered, special handcarts with a capacity to hold 100-150 dabbas are used by 3-4 elderly dabbawallas. For other areas, dabbas are delivered on bicycle or on foot, many times by 200- 300 metre sprints, lest lunch be delayed. The dabbawallas are well known in the areas they function in- be it by the housewives who prepare the dabbas in the morning or the security staff at the gates of high rises, -courtesy their long service in this profession.

Lunch times are generally between 1pm to 2pm and the dabbawallas come to collect the dabbas, post lunch and the exact reverse of the system starts albeit with reduced train crowds. Job done, the dabbawallas relax in the local trains, attending to their other routines. The empty dabbas are then returned to the homes they come from by 5pm in the evening.

The dabbawallas business model works without any fuel or investment in any modern technology, but still delivers 100% customer satisfaction and near improbable 100% efficiency levels, despite great constraints.

The volumes that the dabbawallas tot up and their accuracy levels are phenomenal. An illustration:

- 5000 dabbawallas deliver almost 200,000 dabbas daily.
- Total transactions per day are 400,000 including the return journey.
- Time taken from pick up to delivery is around 3-4 hours and the same for return.
- Delivery is on time, every time.
- Monthly transactions- 200,000*2*25 working days= 10 million or 1 crore.
- Annual transactions: 200,000*2*300 working days= 120 million or 12 crores.
- Error Rate: 1 in 8 million transactions.
- Performance rating: 6 Sigma or 99.99- comparable with Motorola or GE.

Graph 4 :

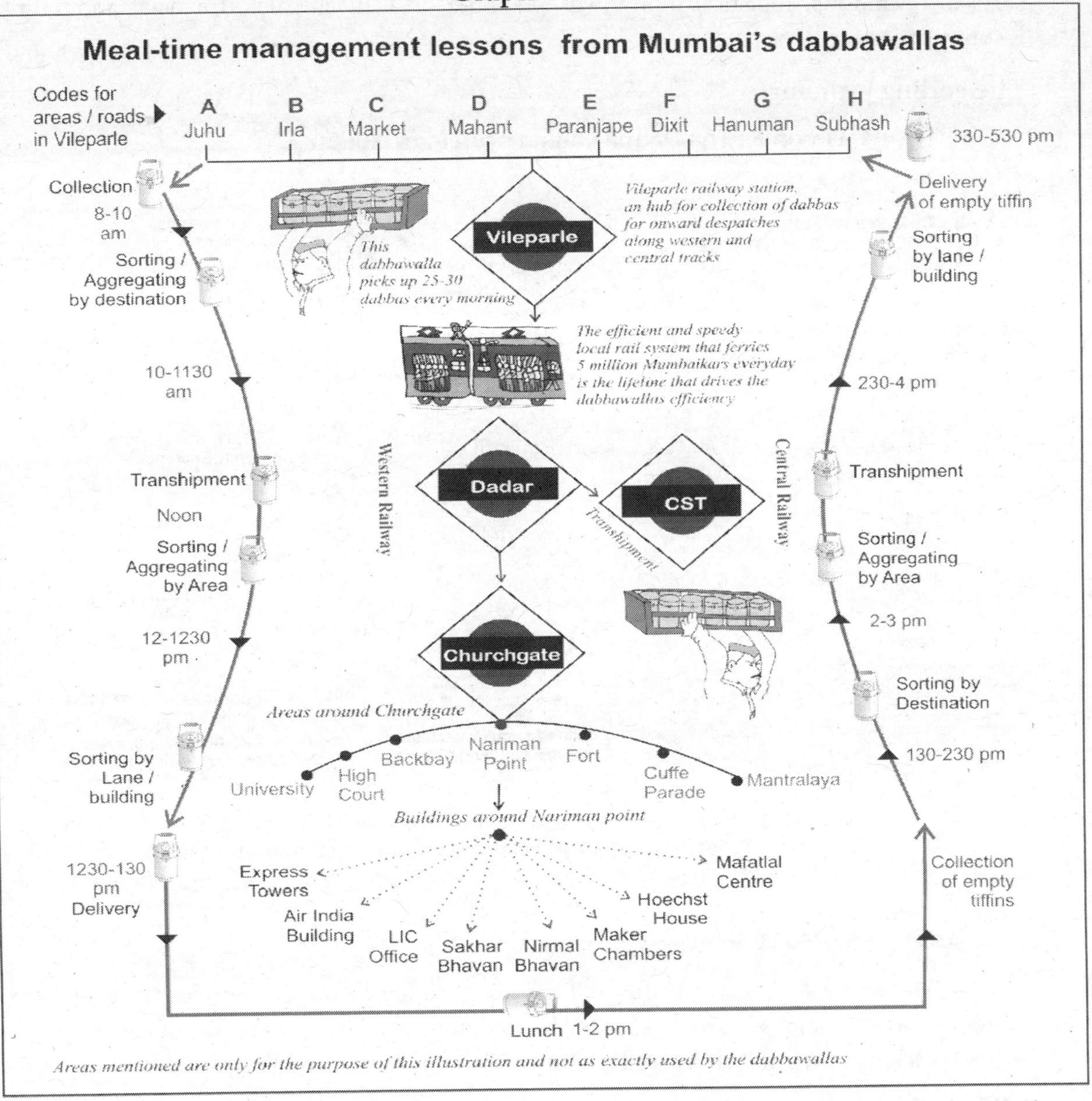

This world class service is provided at a monthly cost of between Rs 250-300. The charges include pickup and delivery, and are irrespective of the origin or the destination as well as the shape, size or the weight of the dabbas. Sometimes two empty dabbas are maintained by customers who have irregular meal hours, so that the dabbawallas delivery schedules are not disturbed. The service operates from Monday to Saturday except for public holidays and delivers, come rain or shine.

The dabbawallas cover the entire gamut of management functions like customer service, operations, logistics, manpower planning as well as sales, financial and human resources management.

The coding system

Graph 5 : The Dabba coding system evolution

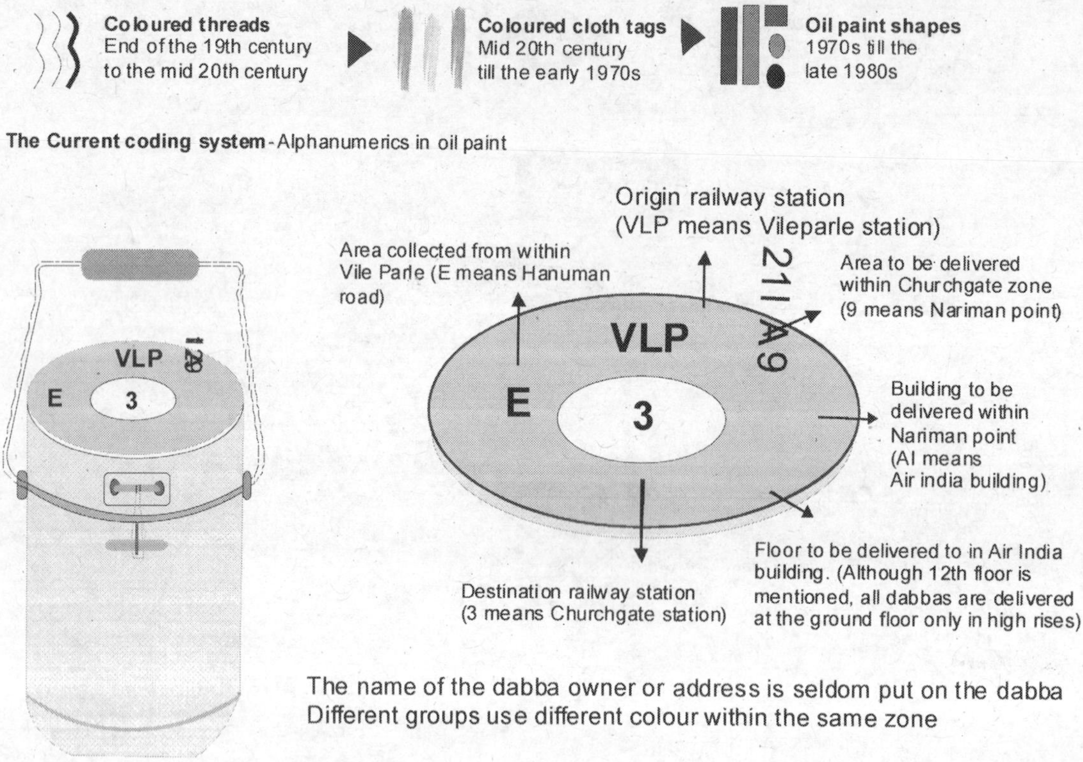

Source : Amit Rangnekar Aug06

The accurate relay of the dabbas is facilitated by a complex but elaborate alphanumeric coding system that effortlessly identifies the origin, destination and the delivery details of the dabba as well as the dabbawalla who collects and delivers the empty dabba.

The top lid of the dabbas is the area where the colour coding is done by oil paint. From the illustration the coding appears simple, but to orchestrate the whole effort amid the chaotic situation that exists at rush hour in Mumbai's trains and outside, and deliver at such a stupendous success rate, demands total commitment.

On the top right of the lid is the area within the destination station where the dabba is to be delivered which is a numeric code, next to it is the building within the area in alphabets and then the floor in numerics, where the dabba is to delivered.

The dabbawallas have mastered these codes and through a cursory glance can segregate, aggregate, sort and deliver dabbas from among 150-200 dabbas with consummate ease. The robustness and scalability of the system is evident in their accuracy of delivery.

Partners in progress

As all the dabbawallas have a stake in the system, attachment and commitment levels are exceedingly high. The dabbawallas share a common purpose and this leads to self motivated working and responsibility which drives the amazing precision of their deliveries. They gel very well as a team and deliver a complex job with great dexterity. As there are no worker unions, there are no strikes or forced closures and hence clients are never inconvenienced. With almost equal earnings (see financials below) of most dabbawallas, there is healthy rivalry and a sense of fellowship, which is evident in the luggage compartment of any fast, down train from CST or Churchgate to the suburbs in the afternoon. A climate of mutual trust, understanding and co-operation prevails.

As shareholders, they are empowered to take decisions at the ground level, which develops them to skillfully handle and solve issues pertaining to customers and operations. This grounding grooms them to assume higher responsibilities of mukadams, contractors and committee members.

Many of the dabbawallas are into their third generation and the pride of association with a profession that their ancestors were into, translates into their passion, without which this system would never have been successful. Most of their customers travel by train and Talekar, the trust secretary sums up, "We cannot deliver only if the trains in Mumbai do not run. But in that case, no one can reach office either"

Financials

The dabbawallas charge Rs 250-300 per customer per month and cater to around 35 customers each. This includes collection of the dabba from the customers home, delivery to their place of work, picking up of the empty dabba from the work place and returning it to the customers home.

The dabba is picked up by a dabbawalla after the person leaves for work and delivered before the person returns from work. The dabbawallas, who pick up dabbas from the house, sort by destination, trans-ship and deliver to the client, are all different. Each dabba is handled by 4-6 dabbawallas before being delivered to its destination.

A dabbawalla makes Rs 5000-6000 per month, and contributes Rs 15 towards welfare schemes and philanthropic activities that the association undertakes.

Monthly occupational expenses include Rs 300 towards the railway season pass which enables unlimited trips across any railway line in Mumbai and Rs 75 towards charges for the wooden crates (owned by the dabbawallas) used to ferry the dabbas through local trains across Mumbai. Net monthly earnings range from Rs 4500-5000 per dabbawalla. The dabbawallas also receive a bonus from their clients roughly equal to one months pay as a token of their gratitude for timely deliveries, during the Diwali festival.

The annual turnover of the dabbawallas trust was Rs 360 million in the financial year ended 2006.

Occupational hazards

The dabbawallas are a hardy lot with each carrying 70-80 kilogram loads on their heads and most walking 3-4 kilometres a day carrying such loads. They begin work at around 8 am and finish by around 5.30 pm. This is punctuated with an afternoon break. Their operations would be severely hampered but for the co-operation of Mumbai's train commuters (many of whom are clients) who accommodate and give priority to the dabbawallas.

Graph :6

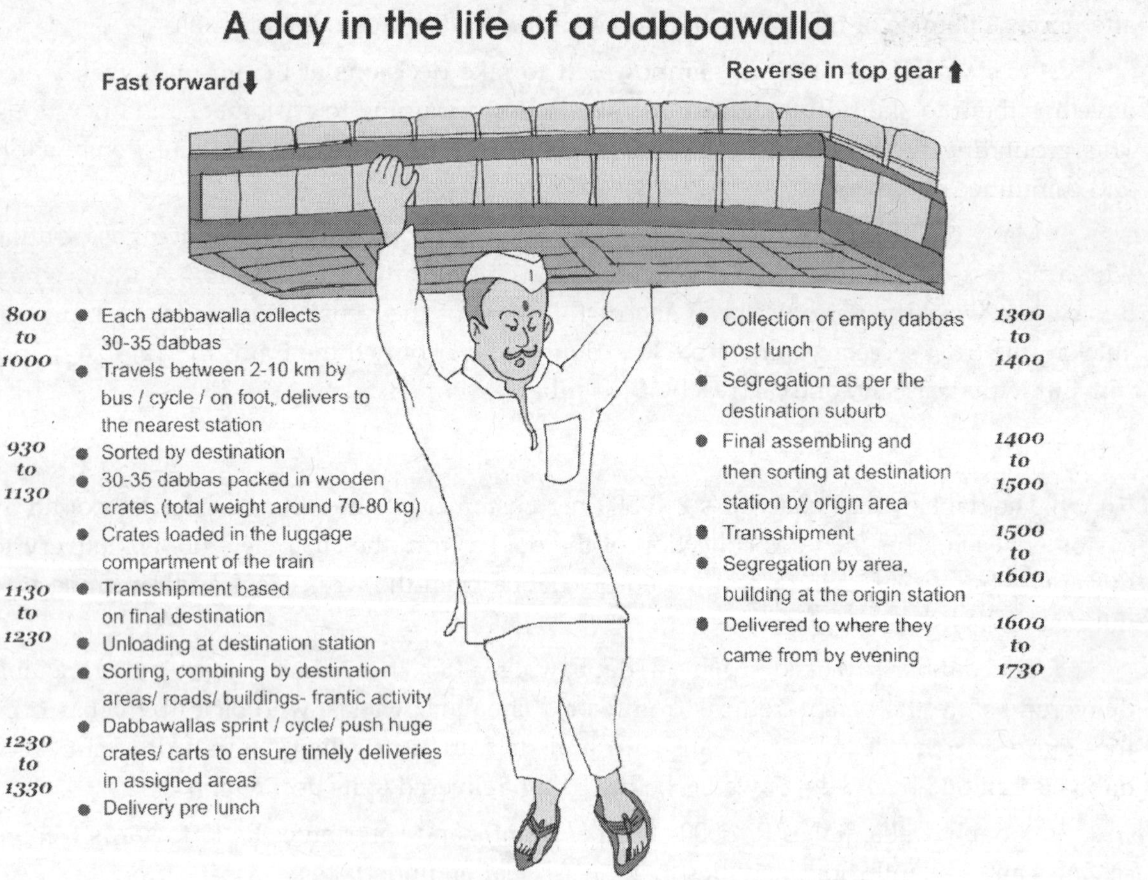

The dabbawallas brave surging crowds at each railway station and have to be extra careful about pilferage. As the sorting takes place outside the railway stations in full public view and at peak hours, there are chances of an odd dabba being stolen.

The dabbawallas lifestyle

A spartan lifestyle with frugal habits and the ability to remain happy and contented with what they earn, are major reasons why the dabbawallas manage to subsist within an average monthly income of Rs 5000. This includes their own expenses in Mumbai plus that of supporting their family at their native place.

Most of the dabbawallas hail from in and around Pune district and many are related.They share the same social customs, traditions and religious festivals which help them gel as an unit. Many of the dabbawallas are into their third and fourth generations into this business and most stay together in Mumbai sharing a shack or a small apartment.

The dabbawallas take one week off during the year, generally around a religious festival. The client is conveyed about the leave in advance and alternate arrangements are made. Their presiding deity is Lord Vithoba of Pandharpur (Maharashtra) and his blessings are invoked before commencing the day's chores. Disputes or conflicts are always resolved in the presence of an idol or photograph of Lord Vithoba, with the guilty being asked to take an oath in front of the Lord, asking for a pardon and assuring of not repeating the offence in future.

Corporate Social Responsibility

For all their efficiency, the god fearing dabbawalla's trust always puts society before profits. The funds donated by the dabbawallas (Rs 75,000 monthly) to their trust are used for medical and philanthropic activities. After putting aside costs for the running and day to day working of the trust, they donate to charities that ensure free food for the needy. They have also set up dharamshalas, places with free lodging and boarding, at their native place in Pune district.

The trust provides money for free schooling to the children in those areas, as well as, renders financial help during medical emergencies to the dabbawallas and their families. The next of kin of the dabbawallas who die or are medically incapacitated while in service, are offered a choice to be absorbed into the system.

Generation next

For all the discipline and commitment of the dabbawallas, a worrying factor is the lack of interest by a majority of the next generation to enter the profession. This is especially true of the second generation living in Mumbai and Pune who prefer to be graduates and get into industries and services that are more remunerative and physically less taxing. There is a gradual shift from the closed-shop system to the open-shop system.

The average age of the dabbawallas is above 45 years, hardly the age to indulge in so much physical activity and one where they could be vulnerable to medical problems. Medical insurance for the dabbawallas through their association is a necessity. There is a need to infuse young blood into the system to replace the proud and committed dabbawallas, and they have started recruiting people even from outside their community and native place. But, the larger issue is whether these new recruits can exhibit the same commitment levels and gel as a team to chart out the dabbawallas future growth trajectory.

Strategic scope

Effectively replicating the Mumbai model in the new areas where offices are now being relocated, is a key imperative. Offices are shifting to the western and central suburbs like- Bandra-Kurla complex, Andheri, Malad and Mulund, as well as to the satellite township of Navi Mumbai. Fortunately for the dabbawallas, all these areas are connected by rail, and the inflow and outflow of dabbas in these areas is increasing, especially in Navi Mumbai, which has an inflow of 2500 dabbas.

The growing tendency to eat out, the mushrooming of gaadis (carts), stalls and fast food restaurants, which offer a multitude of options and choice of cuisines that suit all palates and pockets, are weaning away customers. Besides, many corporates have in-house cafeterias and canteens and also issue restaurant coupons, which is deterrent to carrying home-made lunch to office.

The plethora of community specific local caterers who cook and deliver dabbas to small businessmen, traders, share brokers and diamond merchants, have also systematically weaned away customers through efficient service and hot freshly cooked food. Although they cannot match the reach and economies of the dabbawallas, they more than make it up through sumptuous food, convenience and value.

Mumbai's amazing railway network is unique and no other Indian city offers this kind of commuting speed, efficiency and reach. The lack of such a well developed public transport system, is one of the prime reasons why the dabbawallas have not been able to replicate this model across any other major Indian city, although they have tried in Delhi, Pune and Bangalore.

Many corporates, especially the express delivery specialists have put the dabbawallas model under the microscope but have been dismayed by the low margins that the dabbawallas make. This has been a major entry barrier for the corporate sector into this area.

A majority of Mumbai's offices are moving towards the 5 day week system. This has dual implications for the dabbawallas, who have to renegotiate rates with the customers as they would now deliver for five days instead of six. Secondly they need to look at alternate ways of generating income on Saturdays.

Although attrition rates are negligible with the dabbawallas, the alarming industry attrition rates do not augur well for the dabbawallas who have traditionally been serving customers for decades. Even if customers who change jobs frequently, remain loyal to the dabbawallas, errors could creep into the delivery system, due to delivery areas being changed at shorter intervals.

The dabbawallas have experimented in many new areas to harness their reach. The introduction of an express pick-up at 11 am at certain stations, gives the housewife more time to prepare lunch. The dabbawallas have also been distributing brand promotional material, along with the dabbas to the customers as well as the housewives to leverage their reach and earn additional income. They have tied up with Airtel, India's largest cellular service in 2007, to sell SIM cards for a commission, and are working closely with advertising agencies to realize the full potential of their services.

The road ahead

Says Medge, "One can eat and digest anything, anywhere till one is young, say till the age of 35 years. Subsequently it is only home cooked food with the dual benefit of freshness and love, which can suit the palate in the long term and in Mumbai only the dabbawallas can do it".

The dabbawallas have long realized that home cooked food can emerge as a much bigger food brand in future than any other brand, provided it is marketed well. Increasing health awareness is also leading to a shift towards natural foods and home cooked foods. Leading food brands like McDonalds, Pizza Hut, Domino's are not considered as competition by the dabbawallas as they would attract only a small section of the society who in turn are not their targeted market.

The boom in the retail sector evident in the ubiquitous malls and superstores as well as the boom in the infotech enabled services and the proliferation of call centers, presents the dabbawallas with an opportunity to extend their expertise to these people intensive industries. These industries work in shifts, which can open up new vistas as far as evening deliveries and pick-ups go.

The growing number of private cars and car-pools have also weaned away loyal customers but spiraling petrol prices, parking problems, and the planned metro rail network could deter people from using cars on Mumbai's roads and emerge as areas of future focus.

Epilogue

Meanwhile, Ramesh Kolte finishes his hectic deliveries for the day and returns to hisspartan Kalyan home shared with his uncle, brother, two nephews and a friend- all professional dabbawallas for generations and hailing from the same native place. They mull the day's proceedings over cups of tea and later share a frugal dinner of "Bhakri and thecha", staple diet of the dabbawallas of Mumbai.

As Ramesh Kolte retires for the night on his chatai (a thin mat), oblivious of the emerging challenges, he dreams of his family 160 kilometers away in Pune district and a sweet smile crosses his lips. But suddenly, the thought of tomorrow and the responsibility of 35 dabba collections including Urmila Pandit's, crosses his mind and lulls him into deep slumber. Even at 52 years of age, the challenge and satisfaction of delivering meals on time excites Kolte, a trait typical to the dabbawallas of Mumbai, passion and precision personified.

This is exactly the reason for the confidence that Raghunath Medge, the trust president, exudes when asked about the challenges ahead "Sure, some clients may move away, but children will continue to go to school and people to offices. As long as people feel the desire for home cooked food, our business will keep growing as the dabbawallas would always deliver"

References:

1. Blue P. (2005), Dabbawallahs from India, retrieved on September 21.
http://www.bbc.co.uk/cbbc/bluepeter/show/dyk/index_dabbawallah.shtml?FromIndia
2. 'India Dabbawallahs', retrieved on September 24,2005.
http://www.coams.com/NewHome/theOutlook/200204/inthenews.asp
3. 'Dabbawallahs: A New Medium?' (2002), The Indian Express, March18.
4. Unnithan S. (2001), 'Delivering the goods', India Today, June 4.
5. Ravichandran N. (2005), 'World Class Logistics Operations: The Case of Bombay Dabbawallahs', IIM-Ahmedabad.
http://www.iimahd.ernet.in/publications/data/2005-09-01ravichandran.pdf
6. Balakrishnan N. and Chung-piaw T. (2005), Mumbai tiifin (dabba) express, NUS-Singapore.
http://www.bschool.nus.edu.sg/Staff/bizteocp/dabba.pdf
7. Anderson B. (2004),'Fast food delivers lunchtime lesson', CNN, Aug 16. retrieved on October 1, 2005 edition.cnn.com/2004/BUSINESS/08/16/mumbai.dabbawallahs/
8. Daftari I. and Palande P. (2007), 'Six Sigma brings immediate gains', Economic Times, January 18.
9. Shamsi M (2003), 'The charioteers of meals', Jetwings, December, pp. 190-196

Questions:

1. What are the key sustainable advantages for the business model followed by the dabbawallas of Mumbai, which has lasted for 117 years?
2. What are the key issues that would determine the future of the dabbawallas of Mumbai?
3. What are the key drivers for the consistent performance of the dabbawallas of Mumbai?
4. What are the strategic options for the dabbawallas of Mumbai, to expand the scale and scope of their operations?

The Dabbawallas Factfile

Organisation	Nutan Mumbai Tiffin Box Suppliers Charity Trust (NMTBSCT)
Location	Mumbai
Founder	Mahadeo Ravji Bachhe
Established	1890, Trust formed 1954
Organisation type	Co-operative trust
The need	Home cooked food for lunch, in the absence of canteens and eating out options, at the work place
Turnover	Rs 360 Million ($ 8 Million) in 2005
Vision	To satisfy the need of the working population for home cooked food
Mission	To provide customer value and satisfaction, through reliable and low cost, tiffin delivery service
Product / Service	Lunch time tiffin delivery service
Human resources	5800 Committed dabbawallas
Uniform	White kurta and pyjama with white Gandhi cap
Technology	Nil
Fuel	Nil
Investment	Nil
Industrial relations	No strike in the last 115 years of operations
Shareholders	5800 dabbawallas and mukadams (supervisors)
Organisational structure	3 tiered- Apex committee-mukadams-dabbawallas
Customer profile	Working class and small businessmen
Customer segment	People who travel within Mumbai for work
Target segment	Work goers who prefer home cooked food
Customer satisfaction	100%
Output	Daily 200,000 dabbas delivered / 400,000 transactions including returns
Performance	1 error in 6 million transactions (Six Sigma)
Positioning	Reliable low cost service for delivering home cooked food
Pricing -	Rs 300 ($7) / dabba delivered anywhere in Mumbai -Origin, destination, size, shape and weight no bar
Promotion	Word of mouth and now the media
Branding	The legacy of trust built across generations
Distribution	Dabba delivery service across Mumbai, Thane, Navi Mumbai and Raigad
Reach	20 million Mumbaikars
Key facilitator	Mumbai's efficient local railway system- a train every 3-4 minutes
Business focus	Consistency, precision, extend operations in new business districts

Operating cycle	Dabba collection, transportation, delivery, pick-up and return in 6-8 hours
Area of operations	100 kms to the east, north and south of Mumbai- both ways
Individual Productivity	30-35 dabbas collected, delivered and returned / dabbawalla
Differentiation	Dedicated dabba delivery system
Buyer behaviour	Preferences shifting due to increased eating out options
Key players	Committed dabbawallas
Key facilitators	Mumbai's rail network, the housewife, train commuters,